we heal together

BOOKS BY MICHELLE CASSANDRA JOHNSON

*Finding Refuge: Heart Work for
Healing Collective Grief*

*Skill in Action: Radicalizing Your
Yoga Practice to Create a Just World*

we heal together

RITUALS AND PRACTICES FOR BUILDING COMMUNITY AND CONNECTION

Michelle Cassandra Johnson

Foreword by Vivette Jeffries-Logan

SHAMBHALA

Shambhala Publications, Inc.
2129 13th Street
Boulder, Colorado 80302
www.shambhala.com

Cover art: Erin Robinson
Interior illustrations: Ivan Moy
Cover and interior design: Kate E. White

9 8 7 6 5 4 3 2 1

First Edition
Printed in Canada

Shambhala Publications makes every
effort to print on acid-free, recycled paper.
Shambhala Publications is distributed worldwide
by Penguin Random House, Inc., and its subsidiaries.

LIBRARY OF CONGRESS CATALOGING-IN-PUBLICATION DATA
Names: Johnson, Michelle (Michelle Cassandra), author.
Title: We heal together: rituals and practices for building community and
connection / Michelle Cassandra Johnson; foreword by Vivette Jeffries-Logan.
Description: First edition. | Boulder, Colorado: Shambhala,
[2023] | Includes bibliographic references.
Identifiers: LCCN 2022038522 | ISBN 9781645471073 (trade paperback)
Subjects: LCSH: Grief—Religious aspects. | Grief—Social aspects. |
Communities—Religious aspects. | Communities. | Healing—
Religious aspects. | Healing—Social aspects.
Classification: LCC BL65.B47 J643 2023 | DDC 204/.42—dc23/eng20221110
LC record available at https://lccn.loc.gov/2022038522

We Heal Together: Rituals and Practices for Building Community and Connection is dedicated to the wise old ones. The groves of trees, honeybee hives, pods of whales, herds of elephants, bear clans, and lion's prides. The ones who moved on this earth before we, as we are now, were even thought of. The wisdom keepers who held reverence for all living beings, past, present, and future. *We Heal Together* is dedicated to all who have known that the only way to heal is to heal in communion with the entire world.

CONTENTS

FOREWORD

When Michelle asked me if I would consider writing the foreword for her book, I immediately replied, "Yes, I'm honored by your ask." We have worked, laughed, cried, and held healing space for others and each other for years, so she understood when I shared with her that I am not a writer; I write when the words come. It took a while for the words to come.

I come from a People, a Culture, that uses story to share, illustrate, and convey our history, lessons, and wisdom. It is how I chose to write this foreword.

Wait!

What?!

These are the two words I spoke into the darkness of a bitterly cold January morning at 1:25.

I had awoken out of a deep sleep, and despite my practice of no longer checking my phone after 10 p.m., I picked it up and opened Facebook.

And there it was, post after post after post about the death of a young Indigenous person in our larger North Carolina Indigenous community. I have known his father since he was ten years old.

He was three years younger than my older child and two years older than my younger child.

I then sat alone. Stunned. Heart racing. Confused. Alone with my confusion, questions, emotions, a mother's grief.

I tried to close my eyes and drift back into sleep, but a mother's grief.

1:43 a.m.: I received notification of a message on Facebook Messenger. My nephew on the West Coast asked what happened to the young person. We connected during what I know as the Holy Hours, and we no longer felt alone.

I was taught and know that healing is not either-or. It is both-and. There is healing that requires individual work; work that we must do alone, with the understanding that though we are alone in our work, we are held in prayer, support, light, and love by our community. Then there is work that requires us to show up in community—communal healing. We are each other's strength, sacred witnesses, accountability partners, and healing balm. Sometimes it may look like an intentional gathering; at other times, it may happen via a phone call or text. What matters is that we show up for each other.

Later on, that same day, I was on a group message with two of my beloved sisters about the loss of the young person earlier that day. I asked and was given permission to share some of their wisdom with the readers of Michelle's book, *Finding Refuge: Heart Work for Healing Collective Grief.*

One sister wrote:

Thoughts today that I don't know who else to share with (mostly rhetorical but interested to see if it's just me): Is it just me who feels such sadness and heaviness for a loss in {our} community even if I didn't know the person that well? Is it one of those "blessing and a curse" things to be blessed with community connection, but it also means we hear of and experience that much more loss?

I replied with my experience in a meeting that morning. My grief was palpable, yet there was a discussion about moving forward with the meeting.

To which she replied, "Thank you so much for sharing, Vivette. I do not feel so alone in this, and it's comforting to know that this is not just something I experience."

Our other Sister shared these medicine words:

Something being felt about how we are each other's fabric ... and necessary ... everyone with purpose and nourishing the whole ... with one loss, that person reverberates to everyone— all they carried, all they would carry, the vibrancy their breath offers to everyone ... the whole shape of community and possibilities change ... when a person is more than an individual, like an organ vital to a body (community).

Also knowing, because loss and grief are not strangers to us, when we grieve— really grieve openly/ together, their spirit medicine becomes a force of power on the whole, urging us to appreciate the gift of time in new ways without their passing we couldn't quite see.

If we do not grieve, and let others witness, the transformative gift of loss is held hostage and the spirit medicine of that person is never fully honored across time and the whole.

Grief is honoring the relationship, too.

It's peculiar how in today's society, grief happens behind closed doors, if at all. And how in many Indigenous societies historically, grief was/is highly visible. When you cut all your hair off, that is not subtle, and all that process represents.

That person's loss literally changes the shape of you and so much more.

As I read each message, tears streamed down my face, and I received another message from my nephew that I shared with my Sisters: "My nephew is offering tobacco and prayers into the Puget Sound. An Eagle, Great Blue Heron, Pileated Woodpecker, and a Seal have joined them in the prayers."

Sisters replied, "Powerful ... All relations are circling."

In sharing our words, none of us (my nephew, sisters, or me) had to carry our grief alone. We gathered, albeit electronically, but we gathered, shared, and witnessed with and for each other and thereby eased the heaviness of grieving in isolation.

This is but one story of the power of relationships, of community—the power of healing in community.

My healing is connected to yours. Your healing is connected to mine. We heal in community.

I will close with a powerful reminder from one of my Elders. He says, "We are each other's medicine."

—VIVETTE JEFFRIES-LOGAN

(*Kanahabnen Tabunitckia* translation: "*Morning Star*")

A citizen of the Occaneechi Band of the Saponi Nation (OBSN)

Founding Partner of Biwa Consulting and Emergent Equity

ACKNOWLEDGMENTS

As always, I want to acknowledge my ancestors, in particular my great-grandmother, Angie; my grandmother, Dorothy; my friend, beloved, and former colleague, Cynthia Brown; and the honeybees. During the process of writing *We Heal Together: Rituals and Practices for Building Community and Connection*, you all weaved your magic into my psyche and heart and moved that magic out through my hands and into the stories and words that are contained in this book. Angie, I went to visit your grave after years of not visiting you. My mother and I walked around for almost two hours searching for you; your son, Fred; your daughter, Frances; her daughter, Mary Ann; and your daughter-in-law, Dorothy. When we found you, I was smiling from ear to ear because I felt you and knew you were largely responsible for manifesting the magic that is contained within me. Thank you to the healthy ancestors—you have a plan that I trust is unfolding in good order. I trust you infinitely.

Thank you to the energies, elements, and mysterious things that may be unknown to me and that supported me while writing *We Heal Together*. I believe in the mystery and what I cannot see or touch. There are parts of writing this book I cannot remember because alchemy can feel like stirring the cauldron, then watching the smoke rise and dissipate, not exactly sure where it has gone but knowing the spell that was cast will manifest something potent. Believing in the mystery and expanding into the unknown is so much of what allowed me to write this book. Deep gratitude to that which we cannot see but which we trust is contributing to the great change we are and need to move through together to heal ourselves and the collective.

Thank you, Isis, honeybees, and oak tree in my backyard. A deep bow to all of you. Isis, your story has been following me for some time, and I am so glad to have shared it in *We Heal Together* as a way of sharing how powerful we already are and how we have exactly what we need to create healing. Honeybees, my love for you and the lessons you teach me on a daily basis allow me to write and share your story and song with others. Oak tree, thank you for coming to me in a dream via my grandmother and asking for offerings and a ceremony.

Thank you to Charles, my partner, twin flame, and mirror. I've thanked you a million times for the different ways you support me and the big work I do in the world. Thank you for celebrating, doing magic, and tending the honeybees with me. Thank you for being a gentle and steady spirit as you walk upon the earth. I love you dearly and know that you are part of the mystery that contributes to all the magic I manifest in this spinning world.

I have experienced countless circles that have felt sacred to me. Thank you to all the people who have sat in circle with me, virtually or in person. Thank you for laughing, crying, questioning, sitting in silence, and creating a space for holy communion. Thank you for the part of the circle you are and thanks for coming together in circle. Thank you for teaching me about your ceremonies and inviting us to merge our alchemy into a strong force that will most certainly serve the collective good. May you continue to sit in ceremony with me. May we continue to heal together. Always and forever.

Thank you to my best friend, Amy. I love you to the moon and back. I'm so happy we are on the earth together at this time. May we hold many circles, ceremonies, and spaces for healing. Deep, deep healing.

Thank you to Tristan Katz. Each time a new project emerges like this one, I ask Tristan if they will support me. They usually say yes, and with great enthusiasm. Thank you, stars, for allowing us to find one another. I am grateful for your support, teaching, collaboration, and more. I am grateful for your integrity. Thank you for being my collaborator, comrade, friend, and fellow magic maker. May you sit in front of your altar and find infinite ease in your heart. I love you.

Thank you to Jasper. I am so grateful I get to move through life with you. You are my heart. Thank you for sitting next to me while I wrote *We Heal Together*. Thank you for barking at all the things to protect me. Thank you for sharing your wise and patient spirit with the world. Thank you for snuggling up and helping to heal my heart. You are everything. Thank you for showing up for me in this lifetime. I know you waited for me and now, here we are together. I love you.

Last, I offer a deep bow of gratitude to my mother. Clara, you are a miracle. Truly. Thank you for asking me to go to the cemetery to visit our ancestors while I was writing *We Heal Together*. Thank you for listening to my stories about doing magic and sitting under an oak tree in my yard talking to your mother, Dorothy. Thank you for showing me what healing is by showing me how to love so big. Thank you for healing and staying here, on earth, for a bit longer with me. Your heart is so vast, and it shines through your smile. You are a bright light, and I am so grateful to be in community with you. It was destined. I love you with all my heart. Always. You live in it. Your heart beats in mine. You are everything.

INTRODUCTION

How Healing Happens

My ancestors' grief and their call to heal moved trauma through me with force. It felt like their energy, rage, grief, and resilience were moving up from my root chakra at the base of my spine and into my heart, which was feeling broken and shattered. I had just read the news about the acquittal of George Zimmerman, who fatally shot Trayvon Martin, a seventeen-year-old Black boy, in Sanford, Florida. I knew the grief I was experiencing and expressing felt massive and that it was about something more significant than me. What I came to understand over time is that at that moment, on the floor, as I was feeling broken, my ancestors summoned me to do necessary healing work—for myself, our bloodline, and the future. They had summoned me to heal past collective traumas, the trauma and suffering of the day, and to mitigate suffering for future generations.

Responding to their trauma and my own felt like steering a ship on very rough waters—a ship whose journey was always about my arriving safely at the shore. But because I was unsure of what was happening to me and moving through me, I felt like I was steering without a map or compass, the memory of how to look at the stars to know where I was, or binoculars to see what was up ahead. The irony is that when one is sailing and moves off course, one has to tack back to get back on track. I had to go back—way back; I had to respond to my ancestors' call and the task of healing they had charged me with.

The aftershock from the news of the verdict and what this news stirred in my ancestors and bloodline kept my nervous system in a state of hypervigilance. This is how trauma works. It is like a shock wave to one's entire system—lightning striking the most tender parts of ourselves. I had to be in this state of shock to truly understand the work I would need to do to heal myself and see the connection between healing myself and our collective healing. First, I had to open my mouth and allow my ancestral trauma, which felt like energetic vomit, to come out. I had to writhe, scream, and grieve out loud until I didn't have an ounce of energy left. I had to hold pain that was bigger than me—the pain of my ancestors. The pain of our ancestors. Then, I had to accept that I would never be the same person again, that something had unraveled in my spirit and psyche.

My ancestors were calling me into being someone else or maybe remembering who I was, not only for my well-being but also so I could more fully support our collective well-being. This was profoundly uncomfortable and painful. Moving around in pieces instead of as a whole person made me realize that the only thing left to do was enter a recovery process. I needed to uncover ancestral trauma, to recover and heal.

To recover, one has to understand there is something that needs attention, and one must cultivate the space and resources to heal. Recovery for me looked many ways. Sometimes it was reminding myself my grief was real and warranted. Other times, it was connecting with other Black, Indigenous, and People of Color (BIPOC), people who felt as shattered as I did. My recovery included going to therapy and being supported by a therapist who understood I was doing ancestral and shamanic work and that my ancestors wanted me to excavate what needed to come to the surface.

Digging up my ancestral site was messy. The excavation was challenging. At the excavation site, I traversed ancestral landscapes made up of my ancestors' bones and blood. I endured something that felt more intense than any other heartbreak I had felt before;

it felt like my heart was being squeezed and cut open at the same time, all while trying to maintain its beat.

This same feeling has returned many times over the last few years during the era of COVID-19. My heart has felt squeezed and at the same time cut because of what COVID-19 has unearthed and revealed. We have spent two years in isolation from one another because of COVID-19. Many of us have had to reconfigure how we think about connection, care, and community. We have spent time meeting in Zoom rooms, staying six feet apart, and wearing masks that cover up our smiles. We have spent time trying to stay in connection amid political and social upheaval and death. We have experienced so much death. COVID-19 and the pandemics of white supremacy, capitalism, transphobia, ableism, classism, and all forms of oppression have challenged us to our collective core, pleading with us to prioritize one another, practice collective care, and consider our connection with all beings.

We too are in the process of excavating what has caused and is causing so much suffering on and to our planet. We have been taken to the underworld and asked if we will do what we need to do in service of the collective good to decrease the suffering on the planet and heal. Will we dig up the bones, our history of trauma and oppression, and the blood memories in order to heal? Or will we bury things down deeper within ourselves and the collective? Will we prioritize community and what it means to be in relationship? Or will we prioritize our own individual needs at the expense of others?

Spiritual practice will support us in responding to these questions—questions that bring about dissonance, heartbreak, hope, and healing. Spiritual practice asks us to turn toward our own suffering and the suffering of others. Spiritual practice guides us to remember that when any living being suffers, we all suffer. It guides us into a process of building our capacity to see the truth of what is happening around us, and it asks us to bring things into the light that need to be seen and transmuted. Spiritual practice asks us to heal ourselves and the planet and to create conditions for healing for others so we do not repeat the same behaviors that led us to this place of suffering. Spiritual practice asks us to remember we need each other to heal. It guides us to tack back to the past, be in the present moment as living ancestors in devotion to something bigger than ourselves, and to consider what kind of future we want to vision and create for future generations. Spiritual practice asks us to remember we all come from each other. We belong to each other. We are each other's relations.

The teachings in the sacred text that sits atop my desk all the time, the Bhagavad Gita, have taught me that all we do in this world must be in service of God, each other, and the planet. The Bhagavad Gita has taught me that we are here on purpose at this time and each one of us has a specific *dharma* (duty) to fulfill as part of our karmic path, and I would say, our karmic healing. Our karma and healing are intertwined, and the work we do in this world in service of something bigger than ourselves is as well. Our dharma should not be in service of us as individuals but in service of us as a community and collective. The Bhagavad Gita reminds us, we all contain Spirit or God, and that we manifested from a divine spark, as does every living being. These teachings direct us to remember we are always in communion with one other and every living being.

The last few years have forced us into isolation, left many of us feeling disconnected, and asked us all to reconsider how we connect. COVID-19 and the multiple pandemics and tragedies we have lived through over the last few years call us all into pondering these questions: How does the reason you are on the planet at this time connect with your dharma, and how does your dharma intersect with how we come back into connection and communion with one another? What is community, and why is it important?

We Heal Together courageously calls us back into remembering that we come from each other and we are in community. We thrive and heal in community. It investigates not only what has moved so many of us away from community but also how we move back into connection and union and how we move into oneness. It disrupts the pattern of divide and conquer—of individualism perpetuated by dominant culture. It reminds us how powerful and necessary connection and community are to our survival and our ability to heal, feel joy, and tap into our resilience. It calls us into being of service to each other and the planet. This book is a resource full of tools for healing and a guide for healing through building relationships and being in community.

Through spiritual teachings, rituals, ceremonies, ancestral practices, resources, and journaling prompts, *We Heal Together* illustrates how we heal and facilitate healing, reclaim what it means to build and come into community, find joy, summon our ancestral support, love, alchemize, dream, and conjure in community. *We Heal Together* is a tool for healing ourselves and witnessing the healing that is possible for others and our culture.

As you engage with the content in this book, know that healing is possible, individually and collectively. To prepare for this journey, I invite you to do the following:

1. Review the Shared Language section to familiarize yourself with the language presented in *We Heal Together.*
2. Review the Assumptions section to familiarize yourself with the beliefs that inform not only how I think about healing but also the rituals and practices that I believe will support us in healing individually and collectively.
3. Get a journal for recording reflections as you move through this book. This journal will serve as a space for you to record your thoughts, feelings, awakenings, and ideas.
4. Last, I encourage you to find an object that represents what community means to you. Choose an object that is meaningful to you. Place this object in a location where you will see it daily to remind you of the importance of healing in community. You might also use this object in community gatherings and rituals.

PRACTICES AND RITUALS

Each chapter ends with a practice or ritual focused on the theme of the chapter and our collective healing. For many of the practices, I have included instructions and guidance for how to move through the practices for those of you who are seeking community, for those of you in community but not leading the practices, and for those of you who are facilitators of healing spaces or community leaders. To begin, you might choose to move through some of the rituals, meditations, and ceremonial practices on your own. If this is what you choose to do, I ask that you consider how your individual practice might support you in remembering your connection with other beings and bring you into community with others. You might choose to practice the rituals, meditations, and ceremonial practices in a group with others or as the facilitator of the group. You do not need to be a seasoned facilitator of groups to guide these practices; they are meant to bring us into connection with others, and there are different ways to come into connection and community. If you are interested in facilitation and things to consider when holding space for healing with others, the appendix provides tools and resources focused more specifically on how to hold space and facilitate.

SHARED LANGUAGE

I use terminology that may be new or different than what you might be accustomed to or familiar with. It is important to have a shared understanding of language as one explores the concepts of connection, community, alchemy, ancestors, lineage, accountability, and ritual. Some of the definitions offered here are informed by my work with Dismantling Racism Works, (dRWorks), Skill in Action, Finding Refuge, critical race theory, and feminist theory. Others are informed by my own experience and understanding of these concepts.

DOMINANT CULTURE

Dominant culture is a system that inherently believes some people are superior and others inferior. This system of dominance and inferiority is based on various identities, such as race, gender and gender expression, age, physical or mental capabilities, and sexual orientation (this list is not comprehensive as we hold many other identities beyond those mentioned here). Dominant culture creates norms thus deeming who is "normal." When one is seen as "normal" based on their identities, this gives them closer proximity to power. Therefore, dominant culture functions as a gatekeeper by deciding who has access to power and furthermore access to move with ease as they navigate their life.

PRIVILEGE

Societal benefits are bestowed upon people socially, politically, and economically. Privilege can be based on race, class, age, ability level, mental health status, gender identity, and sex.

WHITE SUPREMACY

We Heal Together is not an analysis about white supremacy or how power works and, as I contemplated how to share about rituals and practices, I also thought about cultural appropriation and how some of us have been separated from our rituals and traditions. White supremacy and systems of oppression play a huge role in separating us from our ancestors, culture, and customs. White supremacy is the idea (ideology) that white people and the ideas, thoughts, beliefs, and actions of white people are superior to People of Color and their ideas, thoughts, beliefs, and actions. While most people associate white supremacy with extremist groups like the Ku Klux Klan and the neo-Nazis, white supremacy is ever-present in our institutional and cultural assumptions that assign value, morality, goodness, and humanity to the white group while casting people and communities of color as worthless (worth less), immoral, bad, and inhuman and "undeserving." Drawing from critical race theory, the term "white supremacy" also refers to a political or socio-economic system where white people enjoy structural advantages and rights that other racial and ethnic groups do not, both at a collective and an individual level. To learn more about white supremacy and how it has become institutionalized and influences cultures around the world, please visit this website: https://www.whitesupremacyculture.info/.

RACE

Race is a socially constructed system of classifying humans based on phenotypic characteristics (e.g., skin color, hair texture, bone structure). There is no such thing as race from a scientific or biological point of view. And yet race is *real* and remains a powerful political, social, and economic force. Race is essentially a political construct—in other words, it was constructed for political purposes. The term "white" was constructed to unite certain European groups living in the United States who were fighting each other and at the same time were a numerical minority in comparison to the numbers of African slaves and Native peoples. In order to justify the idea of a white race, every institution in this country was used to prove that race exists and to promote the idea that the white race is at the top and all other races are below, with the Black race on the bottom. All institutions were used to promote the idea of white supremacy.

SOCIAL/INSTITUTIONAL POWER

The power wielded by entities like governments, churches, and corporations to control people and direct their behavior through access to resources, the ability to influence others, access to decision-makers to get what you want done, the ability to define reality for yourself and others.

RACISM

Racism is racial prejudice + social and institutional power.
Racism is advantage based on race.
Racism is oppression based on race.
Racism is a white supremacy system.

CULTURAL APPROPRIATION

Cultural appropriation refers to taking or adopting element(s) from one culture without an appreciation for or a relationship with that culture. The people taking the element(s) from a culture of which they are not connected are often in the dominant position or a representation of dominant culture. There is usually material, emotional, physical, or spiritual gain for the person or people engaging in cultural appropriation. In other words, dominant culture is profiting from cultural appropriation causing suffering materially, emotionally, physically, and spiritually for people marginalized by dominant culture.

SOCIAL LOCATION

Social location refers to social group membership and identities. It is a tool used to reflect on the groups that people belong to because of their place or position in history and society. It is a tool used to allow people to clearly identify their proximity to power based on the identities they embody. Everyone has a social location that is defined by race, gender, gender expression, social class, age, ability level, sexual orientation, geographic location, and context.

SUFFERING

In many religious or faith traditions, including Buddhism and Hinduism, understanding the afflictions that cause suffering inspires a deeper exploration of how we create a space of ultimate liberation and freedom. Given the historical legacy of war, violence, oppression, socially and politically constructed categories to minimize people and make them be seen as subhuman, and the privileging of groups of people at the expense of others, it is important to broaden the definition of suffering to move beyond the individual. Social and political forces have caused collective pain and cultural trauma and have normalized things that are absolutely absurd like the amount of children that go to bed hungry at night or the amount of Black and Brown bodies who are murdered at the hands of police whom are supported by a criminal justice system that chooses to serve and protect some and to annihilate others. Suffering is the experience of pain and distress psychically, emotionally, physically, mentally, and spiritually.

SPIRITUAL BYPASS

A term first coined by the psychologist John Welwood in 1984, is the use of spiritual practices and beliefs to avoid dealing with our painful feelings, unresolved wounds, and developmental needs.

HARM

Harm means many things, and the way we talk about it is often determined by the context, who we perceive to have caused harm or hurt, who we perceive as having experienced harm, power dynamics and the influence of dominant culture in a specific context. When I reference *harm* in *We Heal Together*, dismantling racism and anti-oppression trainings, or liberatory work, I am always connecting harm with systems and systemic oppression. Many of the harms caused by oppression haven't been fully acknowledged or accounted for through reparations or other models of restorative justice. For example, those of us who are descendants of slaves have not been given the social and institutional power to make the decision to offer reparations to Black people for the violent acts of oppression we have experienced at the hands of white supremacy. As a group, white people haven't taken responsibility for what their internalized white supremacy breeds. Indigenous people continue to have to fight for their sovereignty. We cannot heal unless this kind of harm is acknowledged.

Dominant culture has set up systems determined to divide us from ourselves and one another and to make us act from a place of believing we are fragmented instead of whole. These systems deeply influence how we relate to one another, whether or not we feel accountable to one another, and how we navigate through the world. Not feeling as if we are whole and connected to one another and the planet creates an immense amount of trauma and pain. When we do not work to understand our positionality and social location based on where culture assigns us power or contemplate how our positionality affects others, we risk replicating what dominant culture does—we create conditions for harm to happen instead of liberation. It is my understanding and experience that harm— such as white fragility, police brutality, entitlement, defensiveness, colonization, cultural appropriation, cispatriarchy, ableism, ageism, classism, sizeism, and other forms of oppression—has interrupted our ability to heal individually and collectively. We are all harmed by dominant culture, and harmed in different ways. And we have our own individual experiences of trauma and times when we have experienced harm, which influence our ability to heal and be well.

BLOOD MEMORIES

I first heard this term *blood memories* from my friend and colleague, Vivette Jeffries-Logan. I heard it from her in the context of a Dismantling Racism workshop we were co-facilitating. As I heard Vivette speak about blood memories, it made me think about epigenetics and how trauma is passed on from one generation to the next. Memories are passed on not just verbally but through genetic memory and code. As I understand it, Indigenous elders often talk about memory being contained in the blood and bones. To me, this speaks to the ancestral trauma and resilience that can be passed on through blood and bone given we are made manifest because of our ancestors. These memories and the ancestral patterns that emerge in us from our bloodline may show up unconsciously, and the idea is that we cannot extract memory from the blood and bone. Our memory is bone-deep.

LIBERATION

As with the definition of suffering, many religious and faith traditions including Buddhism and Hinduism focus on the pathway to enlightenment coming through freeing ourselves of our attachments to afflictions (our own suffering) and shifting our consciousness such that we can be free regardless of the circumstances.

In *Man's Search for Meaning*, Viktor Frankl discusses the space between what was happening to him and what was within his power to change these conditions. He describes the physical and psychological experience of being in a concentration camp and his response was, "Between stimulus and response there is a space. In that space is our power to choose our response. In our response lies our growth and our freedom." Viktor Frankl is correct, from a psychic perspective, our freedom does live between what is happening to us, the stimulus and our response. Liberation is understanding our humanity and being able to see the humanity in others such that we understand our freedom is dependent upon others' freedom.

LIVING ANCESTOR

This is a concept first introduced to me by Layla Saad, the author of *Me and White Supremacy*. Layla hosts a podcast, *Good Ancestor*, where she explores with her guests what it means to be a good ancestor. The premise is that we are supported by our ancestors who have transitioned, and we are living ancestors, deciding what our legacy will be with our actions, intentions, beliefs, and how we express our values and what we value.

My friend and colleague, Stephanie Ghoston Paul, has also created a body of work and a podcast, *Take Nothing When I Die*, which is an exploration of what it means to be a living ancestor. Stephanie focuses on the dreams we can manifest, the words we can say, and the actions we can take now instead of taking them to the graveyard with us after we transition. So many people's dreams, inventions, wishes, hopes, and desires live in the graveyard or wherever you believe one goes after they leave their physical body. Being a living ancestor is about bringing our dreams, inventions, wishes, hopes, and desires to fruition now so we and future generations can benefit from them.

ACCOMPLICE/COMRADE

These two terms are often used in relationship to ally, which is defined as a connection, in relation to and to enter into an alliance together. Ally isn't a strong enough word to truly describe what is required if we are invested in deep transformative work based on mutuality and solidarity. Accomplice/Comrade describes one who has an understanding of systemic power and oppression, their specific social location and their proximity to power, and because of this understanding has claimed a stake in liberatory work for the long haul. Being an accomplice or comrade means being willing to risk something for our collective liberation, not on behalf of others but in relationship with others.

SPIRIT

I conceptualize Spirit as a power and energy that is much larger than me and contained inside me. Spirit can be felt through the elements—air, water, fire, ether, on the earth, in the heavens, in our bodies, and around us. People use different words to describe Spirit, including God, Father, Divine Mother, Creator, and so on. Spirit is an energy from whom who I seek guidance and support. I pray to Spirit and my spirit guides each day. Spirit guides are energies in the spiritual, not the material world, who are positive in nature and assist me in various ways. Spirit guides are sometimes referred to as angels, archangels, guardians, elemental energies, and ancestors.

RITUAL

Ritual is often defined as a set of actions we perform consistently and in a prescribed manner. I have a ritual of getting out of bed in the morning, brushing my teeth, taking my medication, and making lemon water with honey. This is my morning ritual, and there are rituals I participate in that are infused with Spirit, such as prayer, meditation, new moon and full moon ceremonies, and solstice and equinox celebrations. In *We Heal Together*, I am writing about ritual as a set of actions performed in a prescribed manner and infused with Spirit.

CEREMONY

Ceremony is defined as coming together in sacred space to practice reverence and ritual with one another.

TRANSFORMATION

Transformation is about changing something from one state and into another. Often, the process of transforming from one state into another, feels challenging. And, at times, the process feels comforting. Transformation is the process we return to wholeness.

ASSUMPTIONS

These assumptions are a combination of a list of assumptions[1] developed in collaboration with my colleagues at Dismantling Racism Works and is also representative of the wisdom I have gained as I have worked to heal myself and create opportunities for healing to take place in community with others. It is important to be clear about my perspective and to communicate it with others as I engage in work focused on our collective healing.

- We live in a toxic culture that affects us all. We are not encouraged to see it, so we must learn to see our culture and how it teaches us to transform the absurd into normal.
- Spiritual practice calls us into seeing that which we have been conditioned not to see. It is a tool that will help us transform the horrific things happening on our planet at this time and a tool that will help us heal from the horrific things that have happened throughout history.
- We have different identities and lived experiences. It is important for us to be aware of our points of privilege and oppression as we make work to heal ourselves and work to heal in community with others.
- The deep work of acknowledging the reasons why we suffer and experience disconnection as a collective isn't easy but necessary work. It is work we must do. We must do this work to heal individually and collectively.
- We are not broken. Dominant culture and capitalism want us to believe that if we consume or purchase certain things we will feel whole. The assumption these systems (who are most definitely not designed for us to remember our wholeness) makes, is that we are broken and need to be fixed. While many things need to be repaired in our world, we are not broken. We are

whole, and part of our work toward collective liberation is remembering our collective wholeness and that we are interconnected with every other living being and the planet.

- Spiritual practice and yogic teachings offer tools for us to learn how to come back into connection with all beings everywhere.
- Our dharma needs to be in service of the collective good.
- We all contain a divine spark.
- We have to develop awareness of ourselves, our communities, and of the world, both as individuals and in community; we have to work together to love ourselves into who we want to be.
- Healing isn't linear. Healing is an ongoing process. While there are certain steps we can take to heal individually and collectively, healing is an ongoing journey and process.
- One intention of spiritual practice is to support us to heal ourselves and create conditions for healing for others.
- We need different resources, spaces, tools, etc. to heal.
- We can heal.

To be healed we must come
with all the other creatures to
the feast of Creation.

—WENDELL BERRY

WE HEAL IN 1 COMMUNITY

In December of 2018, I was in meditation and a seed of an idea was beginning to stir in my soul. During the meditation, my ancestors sent a message that more profound healing would need to happen on our planet and that I would need to bring people together to heal together, in community. The devastation we were experiencing in the Trump era, due to oppressive policies and systems, the denial of climate change, climate destruction, and intense polarization across political party lines had created fractures, disconnection, and division within our collective that almost felt irreparable. I didn't know how the seed implanted in me during meditation might sprout and take form outside of my consciousness and soul. But I knew it would.

I had been in the practice of holding space for healing for many years through my social work practice, yoga teaching, and as a Dismantling Racism trainer. All of my work was centered on integrating and healing the fragmented parts of ourselves. This stirring in my soul in response to my ancestors' message felt different. The healing my soul was conjuring felt colossal—healing in response to an experience that would reveal how fragmented we are as a collective.

I reached out to a friend and asked her for guidance. She led me through meditation and visualization to support my learning more about this seedling. During the visualization, I remember seeing many people on the ocean's shore in California, flower baths, fire, a beautiful retreat center; people grieving and laughing; crying and singing; dancing and sitting in stillness. The imagery and visualization sat with me for some time. In March of 2019, I began to think of a title for what came through in the visualization. The word *medicine* kept coming up in my spirit. But again, I wasn't sure why we would need medicine to heal the collective at that time. The messages about the seed continued to come in bit by bit.

The next message I received was about bringing together a team of healing practitioners who I had witnessed as they engaged in their healing journeys and who had also provided healing space in countless circles and communities. In the summer of 2019, I reached out to five comrades asking if they would co-lead an offering with me. My request was vague because the ingredients for this offering were still formulating in my consciousness. Despite my not having that many details about "medicine" other than the fact I knew we needed to gather, they all said yes. These comrades were from different backgrounds, lineages, and lived experiences. We would be a bi-racial team of facilitators who hold healing space in many ways: through spiritual practice; movement; play; acro yoga (a physical practice that combines yoga and acrobatics); supporting white people in dismantling white supremacy; working with BIPOC people in affinity spaces; working across lines of difference; providing therapy and support; and intuitive healing. Each one of us on the team was in union with Spirit; we all believed in magic and knew this offering would benefit our hearts and the hearts of others.

The culmination of the meditation, conjuring, and messages from beyond metamorphosed into a medicinal offering in the form of a retreat that we chose to call Healing in Community. I believed this offering would be all the facilitators and I had dreamed of; it turned out to be many of these things but not in the way I expected. But the gathering that sprouted from the seed and stirring in my soul was medicine. Simultaneously, I was tasked with something else by Spirit and my ancestors. I was instructed to create an online summit and interview twenty people about healing in community and the connection between grief and liberation. The summit launched in January of 2020, and it was a contribution I hoped would deepen people's understanding of why it is essential to make space to grieve.

When COVID-19 first emerged, I didn't pay that much attention to it. I was traveling for work on various airplanes and across multiple time zones. Initially, I didn't feel too concerned. I hadn't ever lived through a health crisis or global health pandemic. I didn't yet know that a pandemic was what we were about to experience. In March, the World Health Organization declared COVID-19 a pandemic, and many people continued to minimize the virus as if it were truly like a common cold.

While people continued to underestimate the potentially devastating global impact of COVID-19, states began to close, travel began to halt, and many of us began to reconfigure our lives. I began my mornings by reading the *New York Times* briefings, which contained the number of new cases and global deaths. Mask mandates were put in place; I minimized my trips out of the house and to the grocery store, hunkered down in my home, and moved all my work online. All these behaviors—not knowing what was next, the number of lives we continued to lose to the pandemic, not being able to see people smile through their masks or coregulate through a computer screen, Zoom fatigue, and not seeing an end to this pandemic in sight—changed my psyche.

Day by day, things seemed to become more dire. Healthcare workers saw more deaths than ever before, bodies were being stored in trucks outside of hospitals, and people were phoning into hospital rooms to say goodbye to their loved ones as they passed. Everything in the world felt different to me. Everything was different.

The plan for the Healing in Community retreat was to meet in North Carolina instead of California during the summer of 2020. We changed the location of the retreat from the West Coast to the East Coast since most of the facilitators lived on the East Coast, which foreshadowed the reality that none of us would be able to travel during the worst of COVID-19. The facilitators and I trudged on, hoping to offer the Healing in Community retreat in person. Of course, COVID-19 forged a path that many of us are still reeling from, and the thought of being in person transformed into an online gathering. While the location of the retreat shifted so did the online summit I had planned. Originally, when I launched it in January of 2020, it was scheduled to end in April, but when COVID-19 hit, I decided I needed to have several more conversations about grief and the times we were living through.

When the idea for a gathering intended to allow healing to occur in community dropped into my spirit, I didn't know COVID-19 was going to happen. I didn't realize political unrest would become more intense and that Black and Brown folks would continue to be under siege as we collectively navigated a global pandemic. As these things occurred and uncertainty disrupted the nervous systems of individuals and the collective, it became clear why we would need a space to gather, grieve, and remember. In the face of what we were experiencing, there really was nothing left for us to do. Our lives were being ripped apart by a virus that seemed uncontrollable and a political climate that was heating up rapidly as the 2020 US presidential election approached. People were scared, uncertain, depressed, anxious, and overwhelmed. Given all that was happening in our world, it was essential to offer the medicine of a gathering even through a computer screen to say "I see you, I understand, I feel lost, too."

While I couldn't foresee what we would need, my ancestors could. They knew what we needed. They knew when the right time would be to ask people to show up and grieve, not only for themselves but for us all. They understood that we could make space for ourselves to shape new pathways to our collective liberation through gathering. The ancestors experienced and witnessed many of the patterns that continue to create suffering. They also designed interventions to our suffering and paved pathways toward liberation. They understood the connection between our collective grief and our ability to be truly free.

GRIEF AND LIBERATION

Several people have asked me about the link between grieving and feeling free. As I learn more about grieving, the ways we aren't yet free, and the conditions that create liberation, my answer to these queries evolves. What is clear to me about the link between grief and liberation is one begets the other. What I now know about my experience of grief and its connection with liberation is they are inextricably bound. My grief is yours and yours mine. My suffering is yours and yours mine. Your lack of freedom means I am not free. When you are free, truly free from suffering and not creating suffering for others, we are all free.

Many of us move about our lives without ever acknowledging the collective losses we've experienced or the systems, somas, and patterns perpetuated by people that prevent us from being free. Pretending and denying cause congestion and, ultimately, disease. Honoring what we have lost prevents losses from piling on top of each other and stagnating in the body and spirit. Patanjali's Yoga Sutras ask us to strive to balance *sthira* (effort) with *sukha* (ease). *Sthira-sukham asanam*, Patanjali's Yoga Sutra 2.46, is most commonly translated as "posture or seat (*asana*) [should be] stable (*sthira*) and comfortable (*sukha*)," but it is more literally translated as "resolutely abide in a good space." To establish a good space, we must have healthy prana or lifeforce. Freedom derives from allowing unprocessed grief to shake free from the soul so we feel less encumbered by the weight of compounded grief, our own and others. In many ways, grieving reveals what we have lost while illuminating what is in the way of our liberation.

Acknowledging what we have lost individually and collectively breaks something free and releases bracing in the body, spirit, and psyche. This allows our prana to flow freely in the body. When our prana flows freely in the body, we are able to connect with the divine force that exists in all beings, and we are better able to see what is causing our collective suffering and effort to find freedom.

We are able to work to create a world where everyone can abide in a good space.

At times, I have resisted grief and caused more suffering for myself and others. Other times, I have leaned into grief—permitted it to move through my entire being and, as a result, I felt less suffering and more freedom. I have allowed grief to consume me, and I have tried to consume it. We are all experiencing loss, be that job changes, relationships, parts of ourselves, loved ones, or our connection with the planet. We are all struggling to find freedom. If we dismantle all that is in the way of us being free—our toxic patterns and biases, systemic oppression, unprocessed trauma, climate destruction, capitalism, and grieve what these systems have taken from us, we have a better chance at realizing freedom. As I moved through interviews for the online Healing in Community summit, they reinforced the need to create a space to gather together and grieve. They shed light on what gets in the way of us making space to grieve, how grief and liberation are interconnected, and what conditions need to be in place for us to heal.

"Society and culture really don't hold space for us to deal with those big emotions. Capitalism teaches us that we constantly have to be productive. It is difficult to be productive when you're dealing with a lot of pain. When you're dealing with a lot of grief, it's hard to be productive. We talk ourselves out of really being able to sit with what we need to sit with; to be more productive, we actually need to allow for healing to happen."

—JOHNETTE WALSER

"My experience is that grief lays the groundwork for the other emotions that I want to experience. So the degree to which I can grieve is the degree to which I can experience joy and freedom and happiness and actually cherish that joy, freedom, and happiness because of the grief that I've experienced."

—STEPHANIE GHOSTON PAUL

"I think the lesson is that you can move through it, that it won't swallow you up. In the moments when I've been in really deep grief when I've lost someone, it's almost like they say those moments when the veil is thin. The veil is lifted, like between this world and the next world, and everything falls away, and you realize whatever those other little things that I worried about are ultimately unimportant. I almost want to say wholly, though, I'm not a religious person about the experience—I think those moments teach you to appreciate even more. The exquisite beauty of life, even though it is unbelievably painful."

—AMY BURTAINE

The stories shared by people I interviewed for the summit reinforced the need to flip the script on how many of us are socialized not to grieve and not to make space for our grief. The interviews irradiated the link between allowing grief to pass through and surrender to occur, the holy experience of grieving out loud—the way grief can serve as a doorway to joy.

Hearing person after person talk about their healing, which was made possible because they allowed themselves to grieve and be witnessed in their vulnerability, reified the need for the Healing in Community retreat. Healing occurs when others witness us and when we witness each other. It happens when we know we are seen and when we deepen our ability to see others and be with them as they are—exactly as they are. It happens when we are in circle with one another, singing, celebrating, sobbing, and questioning. It happens when we take a sacred pause and ask for what we need. When we are healing in community, the unraveling, unfolding, opening, and revealing occurs over time and in relationship with others.

During the Healing in Community retreat, forty people from different parts of the world gathered together on tiny computer screens and phones via Zoom to create an energetic circle. We met throughout the weekend, engaging in rituals, affinity spaces, large and small group discussions, self-reflection, community building, and connection. As people entered the online Zoom room, we opened with a meditation and centering to prepare participants for the embarkment of deep work. We welcomed them by creating some community agreements and building an altar together. Our time began with a conversation about why we needed to come together in community. As people gathered, we uplifted how rare such an offering like this was and validated them for being brave enough to show up for themselves and one another to explore what was contained in their hearts, to grieve, and to release whatever was in the way of them feeling their own sovereignty and freedom.

We moved through Friday evening and flowed into Saturday morning. As the weekend and our time together progressed, connections and relationships to peoples' understanding of cultural trauma and collective grief and how we process grief differently based on our identities and lived experiences, deepened. We offered various practices—movement, meditation, prayer, and journaling and gathered in race-based affinity spaces. The facilitators asked participants to explore their fears about grieving, their relationship with grief, and what losses they were most grieving at the time. We explored what it means to be a living ancestor, why our relationship with the earth is distant and how to reconnect with the soil, dirt, natural world, planet, and ecosystem. We closed our time together with gratitude for the space built together.

Upon closing the space, I knew the experience would live inside the participants. It was a profound experience of what is possible when open-hearted people answer the stirring in their souls and respond to the tenderness in their hearts. What we created was unusual, timely, and sacred. Throughout the weekend and beyond, we held each other. We continue to hold each other now. The time was truly transformative in many ways. Here are some reflections from the experience that includes both the experience of being in the space and what healing in community now means to participants.

"Through the simple act of being together, a group effortlessly forms a container into which we can safely pour our grief. Just as our earth is able to endlessly receive and transmute whatever we release to her, so the group is able to accept and transform the things that seemed so heavy when we tried to hold them alone."

—SCAR!.ETT TRILLIA

"Since participating in Michelle's Healing in Community weekend in June 2020, I have felt such a profound shift in what it means to heal. Healing in community is a return to imagining who and what we are when we're not defining ourselves in response to structural oppression. It is an invitation to how magical and limitless we all are, should we choose to align ourselves in shared humanity, as opposed to domination and control. Healing in community is an offering to prioritize vulnerability, heartbreak, and grief rituals. It's hope when despair would have the final say. It's the lantern at the deepest, darkest hour. It's birdsong at earliest dawn, embracing darkness and her cryptic ways."

—WAMBUI NJUGUNA

"It's in those moments of suffering, where our sense of self is shattered, that we are reminded of our true eternal identity. Turning toward suffering sets us free from our own internal narrative and allows us to exist in truly pure beingness. In my experience, doing this work in isolation, turning toward heartache head-on, looking at the reality of death, grieving deeply for the state of the world—it can all feel like too much to process. So we get left; we get stuck in this idea of our small sense of self. Turning toward suffering with the support of others keeps us connected to our eternal identity. Facing heartache head-on and holding the pain of others reinforces the deep internal understanding that your heartache is my heartache.

Your loss is my loss. Your grief is my grief. And so is your joy. And what a blessing it is to have joy multiplied."

—KATIE VELETA

"This retreat attuned us back to the power of our hearts, our ultimate tool to facilitate connection and healing. It was a space where we considered how to carry our histories with wisdom, move toward our hopeful anticipations for the future, and tap into our deepest yearnings to wrap understanding and healing around our present moment experiences. This offering created an urgent internal call to action and re-awakened us to the infinite permutations of how we can orient and organize ourselves moment by moment."

—SOFIA LAWRENCE

The experience of sharing space with so many people who were interested in doing the work of jumping off the high dive and into the depths of their grief and capacity to feel joy is an infinite gift that continues to offer its blessings to me. The most exceptional part of the Healing in Community retreat was how tender we were with one another and how the conditions for healing were created through the exposure of our tenderness and other's capacity to respond it with great care. The ritual of opening our hearts so others could see what is inside them was intensely vulnerable. Repairing what ailed the soul and healing it happened as we allowed others to peer into our hearts. My ancestors supported me in taking the seed they implanted in my heart and spirit and making it flourish and thrive, and their timing was impeccable. They implanted this seed not only for me but for all of us.

CULTIVATING COMMUNITY

If we truly want to heal our hearts, move through our grief and create conditions for freedom and for us all to *resolute in an abiding space*, I believe we must come into communion with others. I recognize for many people, it may not be easy to cultivate community. Many barriers make connecting and finding community difficult—life circumstances, how socialization affects us, mental and emotional health issues, geography, resources, access to technology, capitalism, and all of life's distractions. If we broaden our definition of community and have the resources, time, and space to center relationship and connection, I believe we can find ways to connect. Human connection is invaluable, and it is not only other humans that can provide healing space; we are also in communion with every being in the ecosystem. Place your hands on the earth and feel its healing power. Place your hands on your heart, feel it beat and remember those who came before you, who are responsible for you being here now. Watch the clouds go by and the stars at night. Remember, you are a part of an infinite universe. Commune with your breath, breathe in and out. Be in community with the crows cawing, the honeybees buzzing by, and the seeds sprouting in the dark. Commune with inspiring teachings, different artists, poets, and musicians. We are in community with everything and everyone.

PRACTICE

All My Relations

For this practice, I invite you to map your community and relations.

The intention is for you to remember all the connections and support systems.

For this practice, you will want to have your journal and the object you chose for this journey nearby.

Find a comfortable way to be in your body. You can sit, stand, or lie down. Make sure you are well supported with any pillows, blankets, or any props you might need.

Take a moment to center and settle. Bring your awareness to your breath, and as you do, begin to deepen and lengthen your breath. Take a few deep breaths.

Continue to breathe and bring your awareness to your heart.

As you connect with your heart, imagine a web similar to a spider's web emerging from your heart space. You are the weaver of this web. As you imagine the spider's web emerging from your heart, allow this web to connect you with all beings, energies, deities, spirits, guides, ancestors, and elements with whom you are in communion. You might see people's faces, landscapes, living ancestors and ancestors who have transitioned. You might bring people into your awareness who are close or distant. You can invite the elements—trees, a stream, flowers, fire, the soil, the earth, the heavens in your web. You might include spirit guides who support you, animal energies, or divination tools. As you weave your web, connect with all your relations and include them in your web of community and support. Your web can be as vast as you would like; it can encompass many things since it came from your heart. Stay here for as long as you would like, working and weaving the web. Once this feels complete, take a few breaths here. Feel what it is like to remember who you are connected to and in community with.

When you feel ready to move out of the visualization, slowly come back into the space.

Use the template on the facing page, or draw or paint your own web, and map what or who came into your awareness as you weave your web. This map will serve as a reminder of how connected you are when and if you begin to forget your connection with all relations.

JOURNALING PROMPTS

After drawing your web or using the provided template, please reflect on the following questions:

- What does community mean to you?
- What communities most provide healing space for you?
- What would our world be like if we remembered to heal in community and with one another?

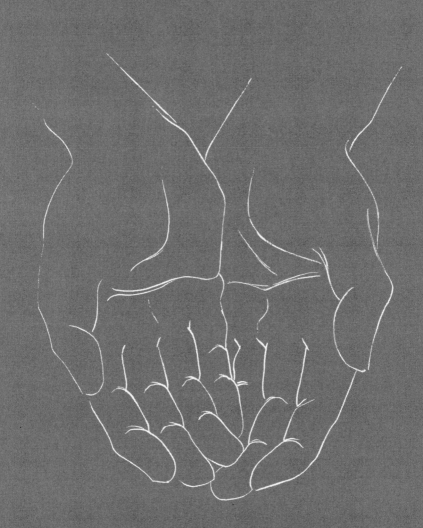

If you have been in the vicinity of the sacred—ever brushed against the holy—you retain it more in your bones than in your head.

—DANIEL TAYLOR,
In Search of Sacred Places

COMMUNION 2

One of my earliest experiences of healing in community was in the church. In this chapter, I offer my own story of Communion because of how this ritual affected me while I was growing up as I attended a Black church, which was the wellspring for many Black communities. As I share the story about Communion and connect it with what it means to commune with others and create a holy experience where we are, in fact, able to be our full selves, it feels important for me to share that I also have quite a complicated relationship with religion. Growing up, many things I learned in church seemed counter to the true essence of God, Spirit, and the Divine.

I recognize that for many, especially groups who have been marginalized—in particular 2SLGBTQIA+ people, there has been a long history of religious assault and violence. My story about Communion is not intended to negate the real harm religious institutions have inflicted on people who these institutions have believed to be sinners for simply existing as who they are. In telling my story here, I honor what felt true for me as a child while also holding the many contradictions I experienced in church. If you have experienced religious violence, please care for yourself as you read the beginning of this chapter. In large part, it is about the holiness and divinity held within us all.

I remember the black patent leather shoes, little white socks, dress, and pom-poms in my hair. A long sidewalk led to tall steps we climbed each Sunday for the 10 a.m. service. The doors would open to the vestibule, and ushers with white gloves would make us wait there until the church organist played an interlude. This was our cue; it was time to be seated. We were always a few minutes late to church, but I knew our tardiness didn't matter because God is timeless and, according to the minister, all that mattered is that we showed up for worship service. After the ushers showed us to our seats, I would cozy up next to my mother and brother, waiting for the singing to commence. Singing was my favorite part of the service and the only time I could really feel the vibration in my spirit come alive. The tones and sounds moved me because I felt God in the choir's voices, sounding through baritone claps that reminded me of thunder.

When I was about twelve years old, as the choir sang, I decided to walk up the aisle toward the pulpit to signal I was ready to be baptized. I don't exactly remember what moved me that day, but something stirred me enough to decide that I wanted to be saved by the Holy Spirit. After this decision, I began weeks of church counseling and education, all leading up to the day I would be dipped in the water by the minister. My mother made a white dress for me that accompanied an off-white swim cap. I walked up the steps to the small pool; the minister said something to me about God, Jesus Christ, and the Holy Spirit and then dipped my entire body in the water. It felt like a trust-fall when you lean back and trust someone is there to catch you. After having been dipped in the pool, I proceeded to head to the restroom to throw up. Perhaps I was getting the final demons out of my system, or maybe it was nerves, or something else, but someone must have gone and told my mother because, before I knew it, she was in the restroom with me, rubbing my back and consoling me.

The privilege that came after one chose God and was baptized in my church was the ability to participate in Communion—partaking in the flesh and blood of Christ. We would journey up to the pulpit during this ritual and eat a very dry cracker followed by not grape juice but real red wine. The first time I observed this ritual of Communion, I knew it was sacred. Believers were tasting sacrifice and being called into devotion to something bigger than themselves. When I first tasted the cracker, it felt anticlimactic, but when I tasted what was supposed to be the blood of Christ, it felt holy. I could taste the sweetness and smell the pungent scent of alcohol. The two sensations together, coupled with the idea that someone with astounding alchemy sacrificed their life to save us and then became an ascended master, was overwhelming.

Communion wasn't offered to us every Sunday, just the first Sunday of each month. It was a sacred ritual that was not meant to happen every day or even weekly. The rhythm of monthly Communion served as a reminder to be humble, grateful, and that we were each one of God's children. Special conditions were in place when we took Communion. Certain songs were sung about sacrifice and the blood of Christ.

DRAW ME NEAR TO THEE
Draw me near to thee,
To thy blessed side;
Let thy love so free
In my soul abide:
Jesus, Saviour dear,
Unto thee I come
With my doubt and fear, To thy holy throne.
Draw me near to thee,
And my soul defend;
Thou my trust shall be,
Until life shall end:
Ever true and kind
To the faithful heart,
Friend in thee I find,
That will ne'er depart.
Draw me near to thee,

Make me strong and brave,
Keep my spirit free
From temptation's wave:
Draw me near to thee,
Fill my heart with love,
I would closer be
To thy throne above.
—IDA L. REED

As the hymns were sung, anyone who wanted to take Communion would line up and make their way up to the altar, and the minister's sermon would focus on us repenting for our sins and striving to get to the promised land of heaven. I sensed that people in church could feel a different vibration on Communion day, more humility in the air because of the nurturance from the flesh and blood of Christ.

As a child, I observed and soaked in what felt so significant about us gathering together in community to pray to the Lord. It felt like a homecoming to come together with other Black people in the Black Baptist church in which I grew up. We came together in faith and came home to ourselves, God, and each other. The church was a place for organizing, fellowship, prayer, and rituals around birth, life, and death. It was also a place that was the only safe haven for many of my living ancestors and my ancestors who have transitioned out of their bodies and into the heavenly realm.

As a people, we had been enslaved, tortured, violated, beaten, and underestimated. Communing in the church was an experience that reminded us we were bigger than our bodies and histories. We were reminded of the fact that we are Spirit and divine beings. In church, the music, ritual, sermon, and Holy Spirit reminded us we are a resilient people and that some part of us could be free from the violence cast upon us by the sin and legacy of white supremacy. In church, we practiced healing our hearts and making space for others to heal. Coming together as Black people to build and express faith that only felt tangible if one was connected to Spirit or if God chose to move one's spirit—like God did when I was guided to walk toward the pulpit to be saved, was powerful. Our faith was insurmountable. Returning to the well of our shared history, ancestry, energy, fight, will, and determination to thrive was nourishment that continues to feed me to this day. Praying for our freedom and salvation while gathering together with purpose and in service of something bigger than ourselves felt magical and profound.

I have been part of many gatherings that felt neither holy nor sacred—gatherings that seemingly had a purpose but lacked a focus on our shared humanity. I've gathered with others and experienced myself and others feeling closed off, judged, canceled, and unseen. I have also sat in many sacred circles and in meditation pondering what conditions need to be in place for us to come together and feel the holiness I felt as a child when the choir sang or when I partook in Communion—the sanctity that originated from the elders telling stories of strife and resilience; the mystery present when someone in church would "get happy," touched by the Holy Spirit and moved so much so they would rise up from their seat and the church ushers would fan them to cool down the fire that God seeded inside them. I have witnessed reverence for one another, the purpose for which we were gathering, and the the task at hand as I have gathered together with others in sacred spaces. I have experienced holiness in many spaces—not all religious spaces per se, but holy because of the things that occurred while in them.

Communing together is about showing our hearts to one another. Bearing our hearts to one another is a holy act. This is what spiritual practice guides us to do, to show our hearts to one another because we recognize the inherent divinity in all and feel the connection between our hearts. We see ourselves in every other being. When we commune with one another with purpose and open hearts and spirits, auspiciousness abounds.

The Bhagavad Gita (6.29, translation by Juan Mascaró) offers this insight:

> He sees himself in the heart of all beings and he sees all beings in his heart. This is the vision of the Yogi of harmony, a vision which is ever one.

To come together in the way I suggest here, with full and open hearts, we will explore some conditions I believe need to be in place for us to be in our wholeness and holiness. In the appendix, I offer specifics of how to facilitate and hold space. The conditions described below are focused on a few things I have learned in my time on the planet, a spiritual practitioner, as a space holder, and as a facilitator; these conditions allow us to be with one another in a way that honors our collective divinity.

THE ABILITY TO LISTEN

I remember sitting in a community organizing meeting in Durham, North Carolina almost twenty years ago. We were there in response to policing in our Black communities, and the room was packed. People from various backgrounds who embodied various identities were present. We were in the thick of it, trying to figure out which direction to go in response to the different perspectives and ideas being shared.

There was a white man who wasn't yet clear on how his whiteness affected others in the group. White supremacy culture conditions white-bodied people to believe their opinions need to be heard and that they can take up as much space as they would like. This conditioning leads to white-bodied people feeling as if they deserve to speak and that people should listen to what they have to say. This white man took up a lot of space with his words, and at one point, a Black woman interrupted him and said, "I am going to stop you right there because I love you." This Black woman didn't have a relationship with this white man outside of the organizing space. She listened to him, watched him, and when she felt moved to intervene, she chose to do so with care.

I am not suggesting it was her responsibility to take care of the man. She was much more deeply and adversely affected by policing in her communities than he was. But had she been listening to just his words and unable to see his humanity and the way dominant culture had conditioned him, or if she had seen him as only his conditioning and believed he was only capable of what he exposed to the group about his whiteness, she wouldn't have been able to interrupt him and tap into a sense of love and care. In this way, she responded to something in the man that was more than skin deep. As I understand Spirit and how we are seen from Spirit's view, we are more vast than our conditioning and what we might show others.

The ability to listen is what guided me to walk up the aisle toward the pulpit when I was young. I was listening to my own spirit and responding to the call from Spirit. The ability to listen is what guides us back to one another and our inherent connection to all beings. We listen with our entire bodies. We must listen with our hearts.

TRUST AND FAITH

As my friend Teo Drake, a spiritual teacher, activist and artisan, so aptly reminds me, faith is about the heart and soul. It is about knowing we aren't alone and that the Divine is within us.

> I think there's nothing that our hearts don't already know how to do. I really believe that my head can tell me I've gone too far or to tread lightly, but I believe my divine birthright resides in my soul and in my heart. And there's nothing that my heart can't do or can't take when I'm fully present and fully resourced and in connection both with myself and the divine.[1]

Without faith, there is nothing to tether us to our inherent ability to create the impossible. Faith supports us in overcoming seemingly insurmountable circumstances. Faith derives from many spaces—inside and outside ourselves, Spirit, experiences, the heart, energy body, ancestors, and natural world. I have faith that I will be held and cared for because the evidence I have from past experiences suggests this is true, and thinking the alternative would cause anxiety, fear, and worry. I have faith because I believe in Source, God, and Spirit. I have faith because I have witnessed myself and others dream and manifest things that seemed unfathomable. Faith requires trust in something we cannot necessarily see or know.

One reason we as a collective of Black people were in church is because we needed to believe that something bigger than us would steer us on the right path and lead us to salvation and a respite from suffering. Without faith and trust as a people who experience systemic oppression, we wouldn't have been able to survive or thrive. In ceremonies, healing spaces, and trainings, I have felt faith in the group ethos and in our ability to create the impossible together and manifest a better world for all beings. Faith has come through feeling as though we are in the right place at the right time with the people most meant to be there. It has emerged from the heart and core of who the collective group is in a particular space.

I graduated my first cohort from the Skill in Action 300-hour Yoga Teacher Training in May 2021. We had a journey—one that we expected to traverse in person but instead ended up being online as a result of the COVID-19 global pandemic. I had twenty-four people from various parts of the country and world sign up for the training. The group was diverse racially, economically, culturally, and in many other ways. Half of our group was comprised of white-bodied people and half Black, Indigenous, and People of Color. I had led diverse trainings before, and there was something in particular about this group and the events unfolding in the world at the time, including a global pandemic, uprisings, and unrest that made the conditions in place for our learning a bit different than any other cohort I had trained in the past. I know trust takes time to build and that at times, faith takes time to summon. I've experienced and witnessed a lack of trust while facilitating group gatherings. The edginess, urgency, and mistrust of people in this particular Skill in Action 300-hour training cohort felt more acute.

It took about six months for the group to move through some of the stages of group development-gathering, forming, storming, performing, and re-norming.[2] This process was tumultuous. In the group's storming phase, which is the phase when a group begins to process organizing tasks and interpersonal conflicts begin to arise, there was a strong reaction from some participants in the cohort about my choice of guest teachers. I reacted with my own thoughtful and stormy response to the lack of trust in me. I had put great intention into forming the training and carefully chosen the guest faculty. Later, I realized the behavior of questioning my choices reflected the times in which we were living. We were in the middle of such an uncertain time, and the news cycle was relentless. People were more reactive in general and most desired human connection instead of a computer screen where it is possible to make a connection but not the type of connection that occurs from an immersive in-person experience. The group wanted deeper relationships with one another, and the confines of our Zoom boxes and time-limited screen time made this difficult.

Six months into our training, a dear friend of mine Dani Leah Strauss, a yoga teacher and practitioner and sex-positive therapist came in as a guest teacher and taught a Bhakti yoga module. Dani is a mystical teacher and often intuits exactly what a space and group need. She taught about the heart and led us through an enchanting exploration of the energies and deities presented in the Hindu pantheon. Dani came in at the right time; at that moment, something shifted. She invited people to open their hearts through reflection, chanting, meditation, and open discussion. Through this process, I saw the group begin to coalesce—our hearts had connected us to our faith in ourselves and each other. This faith changed the character of our group and built more trust, which allowed us to finish our training with grace, understanding, deeper learning, and care. The pathway to building faith requires one to do some inner work with the heart to open it even when trust hasn't necessarily been completely built.

ALLOWING YOUR SPIRIT TO BE MOVED

Having one's spirit moved in a way that feels utterly mysterious is the magic required for communing together to feel holy. I have been called to gather with others in spaces that felt sterile with people who felt rigid and controlled. I have sat in boardrooms with people in suits who appeared to be contained and unwilling to spill outside of how they thought they should be or their cultural conditioning. What I have observed in these spaces is people's resistance to allowing Spirit to move them in some unimaginable way. Many factors contribute to this behavior. Dominant culture trains us to believe we must be able to see something for it to be real. Spirit isn't tangible to some; it isn't something we can see. How can something that we cannot see move us in a soul-stirring way?

I have participated in many circles where we've centered our intuition and inner wisdom and been open to what we may not have been able to see but certainly felt. These experiences remind me of when I randomly find a sparkle of glitter and don't know how it got there. Or better yet, when someone finds a piece of glitter or sparkle on me that I didn't even know was there. They remind me of synchronicities, which are different from coincidences: like the time I invited folks to build an altar together and two folks who are a couple unknowingly brought similar objects: arrowheads from their land. Or the time we ended one of our Dismantling Racism trainings with a song and people were in tears because the vibration in the room had been elevated—by being with one another in space together and sharing our voices—and the only option was to cry from being cracked open. One time in a training, we invited folks to dream and vision together and create a dance, song, movement, poem, or other creative expression representing a just world. One of the participants went around the circle to each participant and moved in front of them in a way that only came from Spirit moving her. She touched each person in the circle, and we were forever changed. The experience of allowing Spirit to move us, and our spirits to move each other, is like no other. In these moments, we attune to the signature of Spirit, what Spirit feels like as it moves through our spaces and us, and we are open to that which is much greater than us guiding us—moving us, together.

BEING AN OPEN VESSEL

I speak about being a channel for my ancestors and whatever Spirit might want to move through me. I am a conduit for the medicine that needs to come forth—medicine that doesn't always taste good, but also, at times, offers sweetness and truth. I realized that I am a channel after hearing many people share that they saw me this way. They witnessed me with closed eyes as I was teaching a yoga class, offering cues and words directly from the Divine. This is why as I'm facilitating, I often don't remember what I say. I am in the moment and want the words to pass through me.

When there is less gripping around the perfect thing to say and greater trust that whatever needs to be said will come out, there is freedom and wisdom. Over a decade ago, I attended a Yin Yoga teacher training. Sarah Powers was the instructor, and I found myself in a room of a hundred people, all eager to hear what she had to say. She sat in the front of the room, and I sat in the back. I watched her as she taught, and it appeared that she had no agenda and that she could teach for hours. She was peering out into the group, speaking to our nervous systems and ours to hers. She connected with every person in the room and made a lasting impression on me. She spoke to us about stillness, the meridians, and the body's capacity to heal. I watched her and thought, "I want to connect in community with others as she is right now. I want to sit down in front of a room, breathe, touch into my inner wisdom, listen to myself and the people in the room, and connect with Spirit."

A friend recently spoke to me about how I hold and share space with others. She said, "You show up emptied out so you can respond to the group. You show up fully present and invite anyone who wants to join you to show up." This is true. As we come together in spaces, the practice of being an open vessel will aid us in changing who we are, remembering who we want to be, and transforming us as a collective. We need to empty ourselves, invite others to join us, and respond to the moment together.

GRACE

Like Spirit, grace can feel intangible to some. People often describe grace as something that one embodies—moving with ease, elegance, and in a peaceful manner. It can be described as moving through whatever comes with ease and responding calmly in the face of challenging situations. As I consider how we commune, create, and sustain holy and hallowed space, grace can show up when we surrender to something outside of ourselves or out of sheer exhaustion. Grace can come from recognizing when something is more than we can or want to handle and giving it up to what is outside of us to take care of. Grace shows up when we are unsure of what to do or when we think what we have been tasked with is humanly impossible, but somehow, we do it anyway. Grace can emerge from a space of great vulnerability and the willingness to be held by others. Dani Leah Strauss, spoke of this and the power of coming together in our messiness and imperfections.

To come together when you're feeling your most vulnerable as opposed to running from connection, which is probably what our nervous systems have trained us to do . . . the magic that can happen when people actually come together and witness each other, and they do not feel like they're in a good place.

They're not polished; they're raw, and they're vulnerable, and they're hurting, and they're ready to be held.[3]

As I explore what it means to commune and cultivate space that Spirit moves through, it seems as if grace is one of the main ingredients that must be present for us to authentically be with one another, holding all of the complexities. This can show up as someone remaining calm when feeling challenged in a space. It can show up as someone extending compassion to someone else when they didn't know a level of compassion was possible or present for them until the moment called it forth. Like listening to the unspoken, allowing Spirit to move you, and taking the time to build faith and trust. Grace requires some alchemy, centeredness, and humility.

I was co-leading an antiracism training in 2018. We had about forty participants present, and I was leading a section of our training focused on white supremacy and the history of the race construct. There was a white man in the training who I noticed was becoming more and more agitated. As a seasoned facilitator, I was used to resistance, anxiety, and discomfort arising in spaces where we were focusing a discussion and experience on race. Still, I wasn't expecting this particular man's agitation to escalate so much, so much that he felt the need to stand up. This posturing of moving from seated to standing didn't alarm me, but it did make me understand something needed attention.

He began to argue with me about the content I was presenting in our training. I don't remember how I responded, but many of my colleagues do, and they often recount the story to me. I acknowledged white supremacy as something inside the man and that he had been deeply conditioned by it. I also acknowledged that I wanted to stay in relationship with him at that moment and see his humanity, even in the face of him not seeing mine. I didn't enter into that moment with a canned response, and there isn't anything to explain why I responded in this way other than my years of facilitation experience, spiritual practice, and grace. He sat down. I believe he did so because I responded to him with care. I held my center, and I set a boundary. I responded because of grace and in a graceful manner. One of my former colleagues shared with me that after the training, she realized that there is something inside me that is unwilling to be thrown off-center. It is true; the grace people observe in me derives from a combination of my own skill and wisdom that has been cultivated over time and the grace that flows through me from Spirit. This kind of grace flows through us all.

As I reflect back on the outlined conditions that allow us to come together fully, I know there are many more alchemical properties that influence how we show up in space together. There is so much more that influences how we commune with one another. The alchemical properties I shared here take me back to my experience in the holy space of church—a place of great faith and perseverance because of grace and our ability to listen to ourselves and each other and a place where we understood we had a shared experience of trauma that bound us and led us to a place of shared resilience.

Take some time to reflect on the following journaling prompts about the alchemical properties described above and how they contribute to the creation of a holy and sacred space. After you reflect on the following questions, move through the practice(s) below. They are practices intended to allow you to identify what you believe creates a sacred space.

JOURNALING PROMPTS

- When you listen for the sentiments that exist between words, what do you hear?
- As Spirit moves you, what do you notice? How do you feel?
- What does faith mean to you, and how does it support you in building trust with others as you share space with them?
- How have you observed yourself or others practice being open vessels? What has resulted?
- How have you seen grace show up and be shared in a group?

PRACTICE
Sacred Space

INDIVIDUAL PRACTICE

Find an object that represents sacred space to you. A crystal, feather, leaf, book, etc, any object that represents sacred space to you. You might choose the object you have chosen to journey through this book with. Set up your object on a table, altar, the earth, or anywhere that can hold the sanctity of your object. Take some time to breathe into your body. Breathe for at least two to five minutes. After taking the time to center and breathe, begin to connect with your object. Do this mindfully by observing the different colors and shapes, the texture of your object, how big or small the object is, and how you feel when you connect with it. Now, take some time to journal about your object and why it represents sacred space to you.

IF YOU ARE COMING INTO COMMUNITY WITH OTHERS

If you are building connections or coming into community with others, you might choose to move through the individual practice first and then share your experience with others. You can share what it was like to connect with a sacred object that represents sacred space for you and how you're thinking about sacred space and why it is important for us to cultivate a sacred space as we come into community together.

IF YOU ARE LEADING THIS PRACTICE

This practice is intended to be done with a group of people as you gather together for a single purpose or prepare for ceremony with one another. It is a practice that can be used in the beginning stages of forming a group, team, or coalition. Its purpose is to invite voices into the space where your group, team, or coalition might be forming or meeting, for people to share something about themselves via sharing what sacred space means to them, and for people to set up sacred space.

Invite everyone who is in the group to bring an object that represents sacred space to them.

Take some time to gather and to come together. If you are in person please ask participants to sit or stand in a circle in the space in which you are gathering. Share some collective breaths. Inhale and exhale together. Breathe together for at least two to five minutes. After taking the time to center and breathe together, invite everyone to build a collective altar. This can be done in the online space by asking everyone to share in small groups or the large group, depending on the number of participants. This practice can be done in person by setting up an altar space with a cloth, candle, and representations of the elements: fire, water, earth, ether and air. Then invite everyone to share something about their object and what sacred community means to them and have them place their items on the altar. After everyone has shared their piece and placed their object on the altar, take some more time together. Gaze at the altar, or you can even have people walk around the altar to interact with the objects. After the altar has been created and seen, take time to breathe together with one another.

Then ask the group to consider what sacred space means to them. Ask each person to record a sentiment about sacred space (a sentence or word) on a small piece of paper. Place the pieces of paper in a vessel—for example, a hat, box, bowl—and pass the vessel around. Invite everyone to pick a piece of paper and share what is written on it. Go around the circle until every word representing sacred space has been shared. Close your time and the circle with a few rounds of collective inhales and exhales.

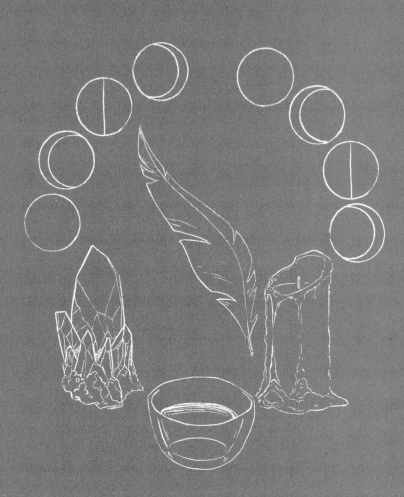

To do a ritual, you must be
willing to be transformed
in some way.

—STARHAWK

RITUAL

When I was a child, I observed rituals around holidays and when one season would shift into the next. I remember my mother wrapping Christmas presents in the kitchen and being sure to tell me Santa Claus was real but she was the person who purchased my gifts. She wanted me to know how hard she worked to care for my brother and me. In spring, at Easter time, she would prepare Easter baskets for us full of chocolate and candies she knew we would enjoy. SweeTarts were my favorite. In the fall, as we prepared for Halloween, my mother would make costumes for us, and we would walk around our neighborhood knocking on doors in the hopes of receiving the best kind of candy.

Sometimes my mother would make caramel apples with us, and I loved the ritual of preparing the apples, rolling them in caramel, and then covering the caramel with chopped nuts. They were scrumptious. After Halloween, we would get ready for Thanksgiving. My family would discuss who would cook what, and we would all gather at my grandmother's house to share what we were grateful for. On Memorial and Labor Days, we would have cookouts at my grandmother's or aunt's house. My aunt always had a fish fry. My mom always made barbeque chicken, and my grandmother made hotdogs and hamburgers. These rituals with family around holidays centered on food and gathering together.

I participated in other rituals while at school, too. We had routines and rhythms akin to rituals. When I was in elementary school, we would begin the day with the Pledge of Allegiance. Reading, math, and art took place at the same time each day, and sometimes the ritual of rest occurred during our forced nap time. The school day began and ended at the same time each day. As a child in school, I didn't have much agency over the rituals I participated in, and they weren't ever called rituals. They were just what we did each day during the school year.

At church, I experienced the ritual of prayer, song, and Communion. These rituals were all about faith and the holiest of all. On Christmas, I loved going to the midnight service, and my favorite song was "Silent Night." On Easter, we would always hear about the ascent of Jesus, which never felt very connected to the candy in my Easter basket. During summertime, Vacation Bible School would roll around, and we would learn a different lesson from the Bible each evening and do art projects with one another. I remember rituals performed during funeral services and watching the women work in the church kitchen to ensure we were well fed at the repast.

As a child moving through all these rituals with my family, at school, and in church, I understood we were pausing to do something different from the day-to-day. We were honoring God or Spirit. We were dressing up in costumes and inviting in the ghosts and goblins to incite a little mystery. We were taking the time to be grateful. We were remembering an archetype who cared about people and who was generous.

While I felt the magic, mystery, and transformation as I moved through these different rituals, I also knew there were rituals with more depth—rituals people participated in during ceremonies; rituals connected to my lineage coursing through my body and blood. No one ever talked to me about these kinds of rituals when I was growing up because we had been severed from rituals rooted in our lineage. Our families had been torn apart. We didn't know exactly where we came from other than from across the big drink—the continent of Africa. My grandmother could impart old remedies and recipes, which can be part of ritual work, but she couldn't tell me what the villagers from the place we originated would do to celebrate a birth or how they would mourn the loss of people, cattle, or crops. Although my mother recounted the sensation of the bloody prick on her finger while picking cotton, she couldn't share the songs her grandparents sang in the cotton fields. I long for rituals rooted in my ancestry. I yearn for the sounds, tastes, smells, songs, and movements embodied in my ancestors.

One of the many harmful outcomes of colonialism is that peoples across the globe have been separated from their rituals and ceremonies. This separation occurred when people were taken from their homelands and transported to unfamiliar lands, and it occurred when people who existed on their own native land were forcibly removed, displaced, or made to be "other." Colonizers dismissed the rituals and practices of Indigenous people while trying to annihilate and force them to assimilate to white standards. This resulted in the invalidation and further invisibilization of Indigenous people and their ceremonies and practices. White-bodied people also participated in assimilation to become part of the white group. This meant changing last names; giving up native languages, traditions, and customs and embodying white supremacy's toxic and horrid tendencies and behaviors.

Dominant culture continues to strip people of their rituals, practices, and culture while capitalism profits off repackaged, whitewashed, and appropriated rituals and customs. In 1879, Richard Henry Pratt began the Carlisle Industrial School in Pennsylvania. Native children were taken from their homes, families, and land, given haircuts and English names, and forbidden from speaking their native language. The motto of the school was "Kill the Indian, Save the Child." This was Pratt's way of suggesting that Indigenous peoples' way of life was savage and needed to be extinguished. These children were stripped of their humanity and forced to assimilate into a culture that wanted to make them invisible and didn't respect their lineage, ceremonies, or rituals—a culture that didn't respect their very being. While the legacy of these schools still exists in the bodies of descendants of those who suffered in them, and Indigenous people in the United States have been relegated to reservations, dreamcatchers remain one of the most popular symbols and icons for people who aren't native nor have any connection with Indigenous people.

In May of 2021, Alabama lifted a ban on yoga being taught in schools. This ban had been in place for over three decades. Although the ban was lifted, chanting the universal sound of *om* and sharing the Sanskrit names of *asana* postures is still prohibited.[1] According to *Modern Gentlemen* magazine, as of January 2021, three hundred million people practice yoga worldwide while the Indian and African peoples from which Hatha, Ashtanga, Iyengar, and Kemetic yoga originate are largely unrepresented in the industry.[2] Oppressive immigration policies against people from Latin America continue to be legislated while many celebrate Cinco de Mayo and the Day of the Dead having no connection to the people or places from where these rituals and holidays originate.

In addition to appropriation, the stripping away of important connections to one's home culture, customs, rituals, and country happened by physically making people change their appearance. In 2018, the US Supreme Court refused to hear the case of Chastity Jones, a Black woman who suffered racial discrimination when a job offer was rescinded because Chastity wouldn't cut off her dreadlocks. When Chastity inquired about why the job offer was rescinded, the human resources manager told her, "They tend to get messy, although I'm not saying yours are, but you know what I'm talking about."[3] This is one of many times when Black women have been discriminated against because of their choice to wear their hair in natural styles. In December 2018, Andrew Johnson was forced to cut off his dreadlocks before a wrestling match because the referee said his hair wasn't compliant with league regulations. Dreadlocks are not only worn in the Black community. There is a history of dreadlocks having been worn in Greece, Egypt, India, and Africa. They became popularized in the 1970s because of Bob Marley. To him, dreadlocks represented a connection to Africa and a rejection of the West. To some, they represent a direct connection to God.

Often organizations and institutions in the US observe Christian holidays, such as Christmas and Easter, while holidays connected to other faith traditions such as Ramadan or Rosh Hashanah aren't celebrated. If they are, often, it is through superficial attempts to show appreciation for a culture without a deep expression or value for it. In the US, people of different faiths other than Christian often must take time off from work to observe their holidays and engage in cultural traditions and customs. In some institutions and organizations, people from cultures other than what is deemed American culture are sometimes labeled as exotic and continue to be othered for not fitting into the dominant narrative of what or who is normal.

The outcome of so many of us having had rituals, practices, and traditions stripped away and not be passed down throughout generations and time is that rituals become a performative practice. Many of us may be searching for something that will connect us to our lineage, even if it isn't our own. My friend Sherene Cauley, a health and wellness coach and spiritual teacher and practitioner, believes that "American culture is asking us to do things with our bodies that aren't in connection with our spirit. People are coming in and doing all the stuff but their bodies aren't yet ready. The heart puts off a frequency. The frequency can help another person regulate and sometimes, people's frequency is off or jumbled. For me, as much as I know we need to perform ritual and ceremony together, the relevancy is important to helping everyone's heart frequencies to be in balance so they can be in a ritual that isn't just performative." She defines ritual as, "an action performed by our body in connection with our spirit." We might perform a ritual at first because it is new to us, and we aren't sure why all the components or ingredients for the ritual are in place. If we continue to perform rituals disconnected from our bodies, spirits, and the Spirit that is bigger than us, we don't come closer to our lineage; we move away from it.

I have sat in many spaces and been invited to engage the elements, sing songs, say prayers, and work with various divination tools. Many of these spaces have felt hollow because the people who were leading rituals in these spaces didn't take time to share the intention of the rituals. They didn't share the importance of the ritual or from where it came. Capitalism sells us tarot decks, crystals, potions, tinctures, medicines, and spells that can be transformative, but as long as profit is prioritized in ritual practice, we have no real connection to these items and the transformative powers of these things are limited.

The first time I had a friend offer ceremony to me was during the summer of 2013. This was after everything had fallen apart, and the trauma, grief, and Post Traumatic Stress Disorder (PTSD) due to the unrelenting nature of white supremacy were churning inside me. My dear friend, Vivette Jeffries-Logan, came over to my house to offer support and protection. Vivette is an amazing teacher and facilitator who creates healing space with and for others. She is a citizen of the Occaneechi Band of the Saponi Nation (OBSN), the Indigenous people of Orange, Alamance, and Caswell counties in North Carolina. I had worked with her for years as a Dismantling Racism trainer and seen how she brought ceremony into our trainings and offerings, but this was the first time she offered ceremony to me. She came carrying a red cloth, mirror, crystals, white sage, hawk feathers, and a medicine bag.

She smudged my house, then we settled on the back porch where she smudged me. I remember the smell of the sage and breeze on my skin from the fanning of the hawk feather. We sat down, and Vivette began to ask me a series of questions. I don't remember what they were, but I remember they were inviting me to go deeper into my grief and consider what coming back into wholeness might feel like. She opened the red cloth on the table and placed the mirror on top. She pulled out crystals of all kinds. The one I remember the most was the smoky quartz. It was translucent gray and the size of a large lima bean. She placed the crystals on the mirror to amplify their charge and energy. Then she explained what each crystal meant and how to use them.

This ceremony felt intimate and specific to my heart and what I needed to heal. After that time in my life, I witnessed Vivette offer ceremonies to others and lead ceremonies of which I was a part. My experience with her and the ceremony she led me through was like no other experience I had before. Bringing in elements of the earth, crystals, and sage, the energy of hawk medicine, the red cloth connected to blood and life force, and her own energy made me want to know more about rituals and how to truly practice and be in ceremony with myself and others. Over the years, I have held on to the gifts she offered to me, and I've returned to her generosity and the skill she has of holding my tenderness while urging me to go deeper into my own healing process.

Vivette offered gifts from her lineage that felt resonant, and I continue to search for rituals from my lineage because it feels important for me to know where I am from and what practices my ancestors used for healing. This information has been difficult to find, especially because my living ancestors aren't able to share much about our origin story or the places we come from. Recently, I found out I am 72 percent West African—specifically Nigerian, and 20 percent Irish. My African roots didn't surprise me, but the Irish roots certainly made me curious about the mixing that occurred in my bloodline. I have even been to Ireland and fell in love with it almost as much as when I set foot in a Maasai village in Kenya. I've always been drawn to Celtic rituals—Samhain on Halloween, St. Brigid's Day, the solstices and equinoxes, and Beltane. I was drawn to these long before I discovered my Irish ancestry. I've been drawn to the sounds, movements, dark skin, celebrations, and rituals of the Maasai and other tribes in East Africa for many years prior to discovering more about my African ancestry.

A few years after the ceremony with Vivette, I was going through a marital separation and was in a time and space in my life where I desperately needed rituals and ceremonies to heal my heart. This separation wasn't easy; I'm not sure they ever are. My then-husband, Jeff, and I had been together for over fifteen years, and we were parting ways. One day, I was in deep sorrow. Parts of me that I didn't even know were still able to crack, cracked open. I thought everything had cracked open when I was in pieces on the floor after the acquittal of George Zimmerman, but I discovered there was still room for more.

I sat at the kitchen table in search of something to ease my heartache. I didn't have a song, dance, specific prayer, or medicine from my lineage at my fingertips that would heal my aching heart. Up until that point, my spiritual practice of yoga and meditation had felt like enough to hold my heartbreak and respond to all that came at me. I did have the knowledge to ask for support from and to surrender to Spirit and my ancestors. What came to me from Spirit and my ancestors was a ritual of prayer, gratitude, journaling, and one divination deck. From what I have learned about my own ancestry, and witnessed, experienced, and read about tribes, history, and the ceremonies that occurred in villages across the globe long ago, prayers and rituals are commonplace on different occasions in Nigeria and Ireland. I am sure prayer, gratitude, and divination tools are part of my lineage. Prayer is a way for me to connect with Spirit and not feel so alone. The gratitude practice is important because it allows me to honor what I have in my life and what my ancestors have created for me. Journaling inspires questions to come up to the surface and my consciousness to roam. The divination deck I began using after receiving guidance from Spirit about the rituals I needed to practice at the time was already in my possession. I had purchased it two months prior to this moment when I found myself heartbroken. When I purchased it, I didn't realize how magical and healing it would come to be; how much of a consistent part of my practice it would be.

I was in Asheville, North Carolina, and it was routine for me to go to the metaphysical store every time I visited the city. Usually, I would peruse the shelves and walls, searching for whatever mystical object wanted to go home with me. On this day, I had gone into the store and straight back to the divination decks. There must have been hundreds of decks on the wall. I was searching for my first tarot deck. I looked around, picked up decks, and browsed through the accompanying booklets. I kept returning to a deck called *Crows Magick*. It was adorned with whimsical pictures of crows, hawks, owls, and other feathered creatures. It was beautiful.

For years, I have loved crows. My love grew for them when I watched a PBS special about them and how intelligent they are. My love grew even more when I moved to Portland, Oregon, and heard the crows cawing every morning. Flocks of crows would fly over my house at night when I would be sitting outside in the evening waiting for it to turn toward dusk. *Crows Magick* became my first divination deck. I had been using the deck here and there and trying to learn about tarot until the day I sat at my kitchen table, feeling myself come apart. Over the next year, I worked with manifestation practices, journaling, prayer, meditation, and a gratitude practice. I pulled cards from *Crows Magick* every day. The deck became a messenger, shaman, medicine maker, and guide.

Over time, I learned more about the crow and its magic. I learned the crow is seen as a knower of universal law and that their caw is often a call for us to remember to come back into right order with the universe. I searched for information about crows and their significance in different cultures and lineages. So many myths share different stories about the same deities, gods, or goddesses. "In Irish mythology, the crow is seen as a manifestation of the Morrigan (in Irish, Mór-ríoghain), meaning *phantom/great Queen*. She was a deity signifying 'battle, strife, and sovereignty,' a harbinger of war and death, who spoke of the battlefield as 'her garden.' It was said that she would often fly above a battle, her cry bringing courage and encouragement to her warriors, whilst simultaneously striking fear into the hearts of the enemy. Sometimes she would join in the battle in her human form."[4] While I don't consider myself a harbinger of war and death, at the time of purchasing *Crows Magick*, I was going through my own process of allowing many things to die or shed in my life, and it felt like an internal war. I was also working to dismantle systems of oppression and encouraging people to develop the skill of acknowledging how death happens physically, emotionally, mentally, and spiritually because of oppression and dominance. I continue this work today. In so many ways, *Crows Magick* portended my own process of making space for my grief and the work I would lean into with my second book, *Finding Refuge: Heart Work for Healing Collective Grief*.

These rituals were part of what supported my transition from a place of feeling broken to a place of coming back together. While these were rituals I did on my own in the privacy of my home, I wanted to be in circle with others sharing rituals and magic. I was preparing to make a cross-country move, but this didn't stop me from gathering in circle with my dear friends in the town from which I was moving in North Carolina. We gathered together for a year and when I moved to Portland, Oregon, I would come back each month to gather with my North Carolina circle, and I found an additional circle in Portland. These circles of people from various parts of my life, backgrounds, and lineages have lovingly come to be called "goddess circles." They began on the floor of my living room, with potluck meals, wine, chocolate, flowers, rituals, and spells, and they have grown into powerful covens that have supported me through moments of grief and joy throughout my time in them. While personal rituals are very important and can be profoundly transformative, being in community with others is a ritual in itself.

Many times, people believe they have to acquire a degree from a mystery school to engage their alchemy. While having good teachers and understanding where rituals come from is vital, it is impossible for us to completely understand all the mystery and enchantment that is available to us. Through its mining and stripping away of our rituals, and encouragement for us to forget our power, dominant culture has made many of us believe there is no role for ritual and that we cannot conspire with the universe to make the impossible possible.[5]

My friend Syd Yang introduced me to this new way of thinking about how we can conspire with the universe and Spirit to do and create things that feel impossible to us. In an interview with them on my *Finding Refuge* podcast, Syd said, "We can render the impossible possible or find the possible within the impossible." We were beginning our interview, and Syd and I were sharing about how I had just gone on a walk with my dog, Jasper, and encountered the neighborhood crows and hawks that spend time together. Syd commented on how unusual this is, and they shared about their own experience of witnessing something that seemed impossible in the natural world:

> As we start, I would love to also share, right before I got on the call with you, I was also outside spending some time in my backyard kind of grounding before our conversation. On one side of my home, I have a bird feeder. All these birds were up in the tree, and I knew I needed to fill it. And then I looked down on the ground and there are all these sprouts in the ground from all of the sunflower seeds that they had dropped. I was looking at how the sprouts had just shown up overnight in a way. I was thinking about how birds are so connected to the cycles of life. And sometimes we don't even notice that life is happening underneath our feet or all around us. And that these sprouts they've just been growing, they're germinating underneath the soil, but the birds are creating this. They're like, you can bring

us the seeds, we're going to drop them. The soil is going to grow them. And then you're going to be blessed with all these sunflowers. I'm sitting with that as we come into this space together.

I love that you have the hawks and the crows, and now we have the sunflowers and the finches. Then, I think starting from that place of who am I—a being who finds meaning or finds purpose in signs. I understand who I am in the world by looking at the natural world and the cycles and systems and relationships and roles and contradictions that exist. So, hawks and crows aren't supposed to be friends. I used to watch them often in the sky, kind of like battling for space and agency, but to see that coming together as a contradiction, it's like, oh, here's this thing that shouldn't be, and yet it is. The principle of the impossible in a way becoming possible has been the core of my own personal journey.[6]

Whether it be through finches and sunflowers, hawks and crows, your own personal ritual, or rituals with your own mighty coven, we can indeed render the impossible possible.

At times, rendering the impossible possible feels like an insurmountable task. We need rituals and practices to support us in doing this. Rituals are designed to connect us with some part of ourselves that isn't intellectual but instead is mystical. Rituals remind us we are all part of a cosmic plan that is unfolding.

In the Bhagavad Gita, Krishna reveals that he is a ritual himself, and since we each are a reflection of God, the Divine, our very being in this incarnation of who we are is a ritual as well.

It is I who am the Vedic ritual, I am the sacrifice, and I am the oblation offered to the ancestors. I am the medicinal herb, and I am the Vedic mantra. I am the clarified butter, I am the fire and the act of offering. Of this universe, I am the Father; I am also the Mother, the Sustainer, and the Grandsire. I am the purifier, the goal of knowledge, the sacred syllable Om.[7]

What if we too saw ourselves as the ritual? What if we saw ourselves and worked to decrease the suffering on the planet as an offering to our ancestors? We are the medicine and medicinal herb, the mantra, the fire, the universe. We are all the sacred vibration of *om*, unified together. There is a role for ritual as each one of us contemplates how to show up and respond to what ails us collectively. You don't need twenty divination decks, boxes of crystals, a drum, a divined candle, special oils, or instruments. You are a living, breathing, and moving ritual. You are the spell. And in community, we are the spell.

We can bring rituals rooted in spiritual practice into everyday life in our workspaces, homes, ceremonies, and intentional communities. When I think about rituals in community with others, I feel the power we have as a group. Our magic is amplified when we are with others who are seeking to render the impossible possible for our collective good. In the next section of this chapter, I offer some wisdom about the importance of learning more about your lineage, cultural appropriation, and asking permission of the elemental energies, objects, and divination tools as we engage in rituals. I offer journaling prompts meant to elevate your awareness of your connection with rituals. In addition, I offer a ritual you can practice in community with others.

UNDERSTANDING YOUR LINEAGE

While I know some about my DNA and have been guided through various shamanic journeys where I've received answers to questions about my ancestors, there is still so much more for me to learn and know. I seek to learn more about Nigerian witchcraft and Celtic rituals. I seek to know more about the specifics of what village my people came from in Nigeria and what their lives were like. I seek to know more about how my Nigerian ancestors mixed with my Irish ancestors and about the connection between them. I seek to know my last name—not Johnson, but the true name of my ancestors.

As you begin to work with rituals individually and in groups, it is important to explore where you are from and what rituals are directly connected to your lineage. If it is impossible to find out more information about your lineage, I would suggest you use meditation or visualization to ask for guidance about what tools, elements, smudges, movements, prayers, and sounds are connected to your lineage. Just asking the question, "Where do I come from?" can be a powerful practice. As mentioned before, dominant culture has stripped us of our memories of rituals and ceremonies. As we are working to deepen our practice with rituals, we need to be mindful not to further the pattern of cultural appropriation. Cultural appropriation is when one culture takes something from another culture without any appreciation for or connection to that culture. Often profit—financial and spiritual—and exploitation are involved in the act of appropriation. When one can claim rituals as their own because they are in closer proximity to power and assigned privilege, this goes against the universal laws of magic and ritual practice.

We live in a world that conditions many of us to take without any regard for where things come from, and this flies in the face of the true purpose and essence of ritual. Rituals are to be used to ground, transform, shift, and move us, not to further perpetuate systems of dominance and oppression. Seek community, teachers, and guides who can teach you more about practices directly connected to your lineage. Ask questions, do research, and put work into finding out what rituals are rooted in where you come from. This isn't to say that you cannot use divination tools that aren't directly connected to your lineage. The practices in your lineage might not resonate with you, and it is important to think about whether or not they do and what the impact might be on a culture you are taking from, particularly if you do not have a connection to it. Practices that engage elemental forces are part of every culture. You can always rely on bringing in water, fire, earth, ether, air, the above and below realms as part of your ritual practice.

ASKING PERMISSION

A few years ago, I took a course on how to touch into what inanimate objects, elements from the natural world, and spaces such as buildings, homes, plots of land, and specific rooms are communicating with us. Every object is communicating. Think about a time when you were maybe sitting at your desk and a specific book jumped off the shelf and was titled something you needed to hear at that moment. Once, I was in the same metaphysical store where I purchased *Crows Magick* and I was looking for a different divination deck. The Doreen Virtue and Brian Weiss *Past Life* deck kept jumping off the shelf. I put it back twice, and the third time it jumped off the shelf, I knew it was the deck I needed. It wasn't the one I was looking for, but it was the one I was supposed to have.

Think of a time when you entered a space and felt the energy in the space or felt the energy shift. Maybe you couldn't pinpoint what it was, but you felt something. In 2017, I moved into what used to be my best friend's apartment. She, her partner, and her child had moved across the country. After the first few months I was there, my menstrual cycle started to change. It was completely unpredictable and strange in a way it had never been before. I reached out to Syd Yang to ask about what could be going on. They asked me about the space and if anything had happened there with pregnancy, miscarriage, or mothering. My best friend suffered three miscarriages a few years prior to my moving into the apartment. At the time of the miscarriages, she didn't live in the apartment that was now mine; she lived elsewhere, but the energy of the miscarriages and the energy of the process she and her partner went through adopting their child from China while living in the apartment I had moved into, were still present in the space. Syd explained the space was holding the energy and memories. Because I was so close to my best friend, I could feel it, and my body responded by changing my menstrual cycle. Syd suggested I place salt all over the floor and in the corners to clear it. I followed their instructions and swept the salt away when things felt clear in the space. My cycle went back to normal.

Objects and spaces hold energy and memories. Given this, we must be mindful of how we engage with them. We must hone our skill of listening and deepen our awareness of what objects and elements might be communicating to us. One way to connect with the objects or elements you are drawn to for your rituals is to tune in to their energy. You can close your eyes and see the object or element, and you can approach or touch the object and notice what you feel. This will take practice. Just remember that everything holds a specific energy and frequency.

If you are going to use elements, objects, smudges, and divination tool in rituals, especially ones not directly connected to your lineage, ask permission first. This may mean a conversation with someone you are in relationship with who practices rituals connected to their bloodline similar to the one in which you have an interest. This may mean asking the tree, river, butterfly, or flower permission to engage with it. This may mean asking the divination deck, candle, crystal, or divining rod permission prior to engaging with it. Because of things like capitalism and cultural appropriation, many of us aren't conditioned to connect with objects and beings in the way I suggest. This is a practice of consent, which is relevant to not only other human beings but all beings and inanimate objects. Ask permission of the elements and tools you use in your magic, spell work, and rituals.

Whenever I approach a tree to stand next to and work with its energy, I ask permission to approach. If I get a clear no, I back away. If I feel receptivity from the tree, I continue. Whenever I purchase a new divination deck or crystal, I feel into it prior to making the purchase to see if it aligns with me and feels connected to what I need at the time. In addition to this, I clear the decks, crystals, candles, and other tools I use in rituals once I bring them home. I don't know who else's energy may have affected their vibration prior to them coming into my life. I smudge them with mugwort from my yard, tap on them, or sprinkle them with salt. Take some time to consider what a practice of consent might look like in your personal and group rituals.

JOURNALING PROMPTS

- What is your definition of ritual?
- How would you describe your relationship with rituals?
- What information do you have about your lineage and rituals connected to it?
- As you imagine bringing rituals into your everyday life, for yourself and with others, what does this look like?
- How might practicing rituals rooted in our divine connection support us changing what ails us collectively?
- How can rituals rooted in Spirit support you in clarifying how you want to show up for the collective at this time?

PRACTICE

Elemental Energy Ritual

While there are several rituals you could choose to move through on your own and with others, here I offer a ritual focused on the elements.

INDIVIDUAL PRACTICE

For this ritual, you will need different representations of the elements. You will want something that represents earth, fire, water, air, and ether. In addition to these elements, you might work with something that represents the above and below worlds. For example, you will want a vessel with water in it, a picture of water, or the sound of water. You will want to have a candle or flame. Feathers can be used to represent air or really anything that represents the element of air. For the earth element, you can gather something from the outside world—acorn, leaf, flower, grass, rock or stone, and the like. Remember to ask permission first. For ether or space, perhaps you will want to use an empty vessel or something that represents a connection to Source, Spirit, or the universe. For the above and below realms, you can use something that represents the cosmos and something that represents the core of the earth. Take some time to set up an altar and sacred space with your representations of the elements. Place a tablecloth, sheet, or altar cloth on a table or the floor, and place the elements on it.

Once your altar has been established, practice the following:

The body is made up of the same elements you are working with for this ritual. It is important to bring awareness to the body—how these different elements are alive within you. Take a few cycles of breath and take some time to connect with the altar and elements. As you breathe in and out, you can invite the element of earth and notice the ground and earth. Notice your connection with the earth and the quality of this connection. You might notice the parts of your body that are connected to the earth and the qualities of the earth inside them.

Now move to the element of water. Notice the flow of breath in the body, similar to the flow of the ocean waves. Imagine hearing the sound of water flowing or the waves crashing on the shore. You can begin to move, perhaps moving from side to side, as if you are in a body of water, allowing the current to sway you.

Next, connect with the element of fire. Feel your own internal fire and the sensation of warmth. Bring your awareness to your solar plexus and imagine the sun's rays shining brightly into and out from your solar plexus.

Now connect with the element of air. Feel the temperature in the room or space. Feel the sensation of air on your skin. Feel the air move into your body through your nostrils as you inhale you might notice the air feels and as you exhale, you might notice a warm sensation as the breath leaves your nostrils. You can open your eyes if they are closed and connect with the outside world. If there are windows in your space, observe the wind and how it moves the leaves and trees outside. If you are outside for this ritual, in addition to being able to see the wind move things in the natural world, listen for the sound of your breath.

Now move to the ether. The ether is often described as space, stillness, or the energy all around us. It is around us but not something we can see or touch. Connect with the energy around you—space you cannot see but that is present. Be still and take a moment to listen to what you hear as you are still.

Last, work with the above and below realms. Ground through your feet, seat, or whatever parts of your body are touching the earth. Go deeper, to bring your awareness down through the floor, floorboards, dirt, and different layers of the earth. Bring your awareness all the way down and into the core of the earth. Gather up earthly energy from the below realm and fill up with this energy. After a couple of minutes here, bring your awareness back up from the core of the earth, all the way up through your body and out through the crown of your head. All the way up through the trees and sky. All the way up to the cosmos with the stars, planets, dark void, and mystery. Gather up cosmic energy and allow yourself to fill up with it. As you feel ready, begin to come back into your space and bring your awareness back to your breath. Take seven deep breaths. As you complete this ritual, take a moment to thank the elemental energies for their support, guidance, and help. Once you have offered gratitude to the elemental energies involved in this ritual, reflect on your experience practicing the ritual. Take a moment to journal, or sit in silence to reflect. This is a practice you can return to anytime you would like to connect with the elemental energy inside and around you.

IF YOU ARE COMING INTO COMMUNITY WITH OTHERS

For this practice, you might choose to move through the individual practice listed above and share about your experience with someone. You might also decide you would like to connect with the elements with someone else. Perhaps you would like to take a walk in the woods and connect with the element of air. Perhaps you would like to visit your favorite park or trail and connect with the earth. Maybe you'd like to practice a walking or seated meditation outside with someone. Perhaps you would like to visit your favorite river, lake, or ocean with someone and connect with the element of water. You can come into community with others, including the natural world, as you connect with the elements. Whatever you choose to do, I invite you to practice with someone else and share about your experience.

IF YOU ARE LEADING THIS PRACTICE

For this ritual, you can gather the earth elements as explained in the individual practice and bring them to the group or ask the group to gather them.

If you are setting up the space and bringing in all these elements, take some time to set up an altar. Place a tablecloth, sheet, or altar cloth on a table or the floor, and place the elements on it. If you are setting up the space with others, you can provide the altar cloth and have people place their objects on the altar once you have opened the space. Once your altar has been established, practice the following:

The body is made up of the same elements you are working with for this ritual. It is important to bring awareness to the body and invite people to notice how these different elements are alive within them. Invite everyone to take a few cycles of breath and take some time to connect with the altar and elements. As people breathe in and out, you can invite the element of earth by asking people to notice the ground and earth. Ask them to notice their connection with the earth and the quality of this connection. You might even invite people to touch the earth or notice the parts of their body that are connecting to it. Invite people to notice the qualities of the earth inside them.

Now move to the element of water. Invite people to notice the flow of breath in their body, similar to the flow of ocean waves. You might even invite them to imagine hearing water flowing or the waves crashing on the shore. You can also invite in movement. Suggest each group member move from side to side, as if they are in a body of water, allowing the current to sway them from side to side.

Next, connect with the element of fire. Invite the group to feel their own internal fire and the sensation of warmth. Invite them to bring their awareness to their solar plexus, and to imagine the sun's rays shining brightly in to and out from the solar plexus. After they have had an opportunity to connect to their own fire, invite them to connect to the fire and energy held within the group.

Now invite the group to connect with the element of air. You might invite them to feel the temperature in the room or space if you aren't in person for this ritual—to feel the sensation of air on their skin. Ask people to feel the air move into their body through their nostrils as they inhale and warm air move out of their nostrils as they exhale, connecting their breath with the element of air. You can invite them to open their eyes if they are closed and connect with the outside world. If there are windows in the space, people can observe the wind and how it moves the leaves and trees outside. If they are outside for this ritual, in addition to being able to see the wind move things in the natural world, they can listen for the sound of their breath.

Now move to the ether. The ether is often described as space, stillness, or the energy all around us, but it is not something we can see or touch. Invite people to connect with the energy around them and the group and the space around them—space they cannot see but that is present. Invite people to be still and take a moment to listen to what they hear as they are still. Ask them to focus on the space they are creating as a group and imagine what it might be filled with, whether it's laughter, joy, transformation, love, work for the collective good, and so forth.

Last, work with the above and below realms. Invite the group to ground through their feet, seat, or whatever parts of their body are touching the earth. Then invite them to go deeper, to bring their awareness down through the floor, floorboards, dirt, and different layers of the earth. Invite them to bring their awareness all the way down and into the core of the earth. Invite the group to gather up earthly energy from the below realm and fill up with this energy. After a couple of minutes there, invite the group to bring their awareness back up from the core of the earth, all the way up through their body and out through the crown of their head. All the way up through the trees and sky. All the way up to the cosmos with the stars, planets, dark void, and mystery. Invite them to gather up cosmic energy and allow themselves to fill up with it. After a couple of minutes here, bring people back into the space by inviting them to bring their awareness back to their breath. Invite the group to take seven deep breaths together. As you complete this ritual, take a moment to thank the elemental energies for their support, guidance, and help. Once you have offered gratitude to the elemental energies involved in this ritual, invite participants to reflect on their experience practicing the ritual and share about it. You might ask them to take a moment to meditate, journal, or sit in silence to reflect. Then you can open the space for people to share.

Note: This ritual involves many elements, but you could also work with one element or a few at a time. You could create an entire water, fire, air, ether, or earth ritual. Practice the ritual to see how it feels to you and those who practice it with you. Adapt as you need or based on what you are seeking. Adapt based on the season, the weather, and what the collective might need at a specific time. Rituals are meant to resonate most with you and the group with whom you are practicing.

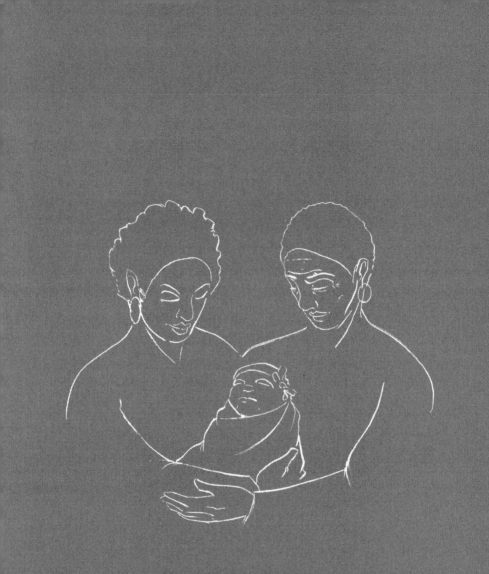

The root of oppression
is loss of memory.

—PAULA GUNN ALLEN

LINEAGE AND LEGACY

Where do you come from?—I have been searching for an answer to this question for most of my life. When I was in elementary school, I distinctly remember a homework assignment where I was instructed to map my family tree. I took the worksheet home in my backpack and shared it with my mom. She wasn't thrilled about this assignment. She told me we couldn't trace our lineage past my great-grandmother, Angie. She also instructed me to go to school the next day and share how insensitive the assignment was given that many of my ancestors were forcibly brought to this land and enslaved.

Later in school, I was asked once again to share more about where I come from through an assignment to create a family crest. All the other children created artistic representations of crests or brought in actual family crests and artifacts associated with their lineage. Of course, I couldn't do this. Johnson was a name given to me through the system of slavery and not one that had a crest or any royalty associated with it that benefited me. I ended up drawing a family crest with vibrant colors to represent the pride I felt about my immediate family, those known to me. Where we come from may seem like a simple inquiry, but the answer to this question is riddled with a history known and unknown to us, traumas passed on from one generation to the next, and perseverance that can move through one's bloodline.

In 2020, I decided to find out more about my lineage. I spit into a vial and sent it off to 23andme.com, a company that helps you trace your ancestry by linking your DNA to geographic areas of the world. The vial sat for a few days next to my front door. We were in the middle of the COVID-19 pandemic, and I was sparingly visiting the post office. While the vial and soon-to-be answer to the question of where I come from sat next to my front door, I had a psychic reading gifted to me by a friend.

The psychic went into a trance and the first question she asked me was, "Who are your people? Where do you come from?" I chuckled because I knew this was Spirit at work and not a coincidence. I ask people these questions all the time. It is routine for me to begin workshops and trainings by asking people to call in their ancestors or to share something about where they are from. Plus, the only thing keeping me from knowing more about my bloodline was the 23andme.com package sitting next to the front door.

The psychic was asking me about my origin story and not just the story of how I came to be in this incarnation of myself. I answered by saying, "I'm from my mother, Clara, and my father, Cornelius. I am from my paternal grandmother, Sally, and my paternal grandfather, Cornelius. I am from my maternal grandmother, Dorothy, and maternal grandfather, Fred. I am from Angie, my maternal great-grandmother. I don't know much about her. She was born into slavery, and she had dementia for most of my childhood. Stories of our family's history dissolved when she transitioned." I shared a little about each ancestor and went on to say, "I am from everyone and everything. I am from the cosmos, the earth, the dirt, and everything around me." The psychic paused and then said, "Angie is the only person you described by the conditions in place when she was a child. You said she was born into slavery and that you didn't know much about her. You described the other ancestors—living and those who have transitioned, by sharing things about them, not the conditions in which they were born into or lived."

This almost made me drop my teacup and the rose tea inside it. I was struck by her observation and the truth she revealed. I had been describing Angie in this way for as long as I could remember. The belief and awareness that we are bigger than the conditions in place was a belief I had held for quite some time, and still, I described my great-grandmother as the conditions in place for her instead of as a whole human who had a life story beyond the conditions created by oppression and white supremacy. As this revelation was sinking into my consciousness, a honeybee came up to my window and flew around a bit. I assume this bee was from the hive, Infinity, and was Angie's spirit affirming that she was present with us, working between realms, and that she wanted to be seen as who she was—a vibrant human, not only as someone who was enslaved or suffered from dementia.

Angie's spirit weaved through the entire psychic reading, and at one point in my consciousness, I saw myself at the water's edge with Angie. We were at the ocean sitting in two chairs across from one another. The tide was moving in and out. As we sat across from each other, I was pushing the tide in and offering water to Angie, and she was pushing the tide out and offering water to me. It was an infinite flow of energy, love, grace, and compassion. This visualization reminded me of an adage I would often use in the past in response to people asking me about myself and my work: "I am a drop in the bucket." In the visualization, Angie was showing me this was in fact true. I am a drop and the entire ocean, just as she is the entire ocean—not one single drop, story, or limiting condition. She was passing the water back to me to very clearly remind me that I come from her. She is part of my lineage and story, and she is part of everything and everyone. Every drop in the ocean.

Angie wasn't tall in stature but she was vast in spirit. She stood about five feet tall, hunched over with scoliosis that emerged from leaning over hot stoves and cooking for hours each day. She lived on what to me appeared to be an old plantation turned into a dairy farm. She worked as a domestic, and more specifically as a cook for the Mitchells who owned and ran the dairy farm. Angie's husband passed away when their son, my grandfather, Fred, was nine years old. My great-grandfather was a butler and servant who traveled with the family he worked for. He came home when he was sick with what we now believe was tuberculosis. After his passing, Angie became the sole provider for the family, and my grandfather decided to leave school in the fourth grade and go to work. He came to live and work with Angie on the dairy farm. Angie lived in the main house, which was a privilege at the time. My grandfather and the other domestic workers lived in what were previously likely slave quarters, separate from the main house and hidden away.

Angie devoted herself to cooking for the family and sometimes she would babysit the Mitchells' children and do light housekeeping. She had more of an education than her daughter, my great aunt, Frances, and her son, Fred. The Mitchells' children taught Angie how to read and write. Occasionally Angie was able to go clothes shopping with the Mitchells and buy dresses and other items. Many of the other Black people working on the dairy farm didn't have this same privilege.

Angie was feisty. She was sprightly. She would cuss you out if you crossed her. She chewed snuff and spit tobacco, and she was a masterful fisher. She loved wearing fancy hats to church, and she would come to my grandmother's house after church service for dinner. In her purse she always had something sweet for the grand and great-grandchildren. She would say, "Let me see what I have in here for you," almost like it was a game. Whatever she would pull out might surprise her as much as it would delight us.

She would take me and my brother fishing in the pond on the plantation. We would get in a small tugboat, and she would put the worms on the fishing line and throw them in. I don't remember if we caught any fish, but I do remember how much I loved watching her sit in the boat with her fishing line, creating a little peace for herself. I imagine the water and being outside, instead of inside a hot kitchen laboring all day, felt good to her.

One of the first times I learned about deep sorrow was from watching Angie after her son, Fred, passed away. I remember her saying, "It is unnatural for a child to die before their parents die." These words have stayed with me since I heard them come out of her mouth. I've often thought about the specific kind of heartbreak she must have felt having to bury her son before she herself was buried.

When I was about ten or eleven, Angie began to exhibit noticeable signs of dementia. At the time, she was living with the Mitchells, and when she could no longer work for them she went to live with her daughter, Frances. We would go visit her every week, and she would share stories about things that made no sense to me because I couldn't place the characters or landscapes she would describe. Her daughter dismissed her. I knew she was telling stories that were important to our family, but none of us could put the pieces together to create a map that traced back to where we came from. During these times of weaving in and out of lucidity, Angie shared about the dirt floors that were in her house as a child. She shared about her mother having been enslaved and her family having been split apart because of the system of slavery. She shared stories about working for the Mitchells. She would weave in and out of story and our reality at the time, and I could tell there was more she wanted to share with us. In so many ways, her experience of dementia mirrored the conditions created by enslavement—a lack of liberation.

I imagine she felt trapped in her mind at times, and at a certain point, she was trapped in her bed, immobile. To me, this was one of the saddest experiences to move through. I knew she was a vibrant being. When she was ill, it felt as if her vibrancy faded just like her mental capacity. It felt unnatural for her to fade away, just as it had felt unnatural to her for her son to die before her. The experience of witnessing her seemingly fade away coupled with how our memories change over time is what, I believe, led me to start describing her as the conditions in place. This didn't serve or honor her but, instead, minimized her.

The psychic's wisdom seeped into my heart. Since the time of that reading, I have engaged with Angie and her infinite and expansive energy many times. I have called on her to be in the flow with me where both of us give and receive the water. She has called on me to remember I am a drop and the ocean. It feels like a continuous cycle, one she was waiting for me to recognize and participate in.

Our ancestors, known to us and unknown, are in an infinite cycle with us. We carry them inside us, and they manifested us. Part of what causes our suffering is our inability to recollect or remember. We forget our shared history, our connection to all beings and that we are part of an infinite cycle. We forget we have always been and will always be. Part of the wisdom I was reminded of when the psychic asked me where I came from and who my people were was the wisdom Krishna offered Arjuna in the Bhagavad Gita when Arjuna expressed resistance about living into his dharma. He said, "You have always been and you will always be. Your soul is everlasting" (Bhagavad Gita, 2.40).

All of who we have ever been and who we come from resides in our cells, sinew, marrow, consciousness, and blood. Sinew is the structure that binds things together, and we are bound to our ancestors, lineage, and collective history. My comrade Alexis Pauline Gumbs, a queer Black feminist, author, and facilitator of magic, reminds us that lifetimes are not a barrier to love or ancestral knowledge:

Lifetimes are not a barrier. They're just these forms that can be a way for us to experience love and they can teach us about what did that look like. What did it look like for that love to move through this particular moment in history? Or what would it, what would it look like given what's possible in the future?[1]

Our ancestors, known and unknown, remind us that we aren't our cultural conditioning or the conditions that people created for us. While we come from a specific bloodline and ancestry, we aren't bound to repeat the same patterns in our line and ancestry. We aren't bound to create wars, systems of dominance and superiority, divisions, caste systems, or hierarchies.

If we are unable to explore the roots of both trauma and resilience that run like pulsing veins through our bloodlines, it will be difficult to place ourselves in the current context and understand how we got here. It will be difficult to break patterns because the denial of where we come from and how we came to be in this moment denies us the opportunity to heal in response to our collective historical trauma. I believe we must be in relationship with our ancestors, honor the healthy parts of who they were, and acknowledge the toxic patterns held within them due to unresolved trauma and a lack of understanding of the impact of collective trauma.

This is deep work and an ongoing practice. In *My Grandmother's Hands: Racialized Trauma and the Pathway to Mending Our Hearts and Bodies*, Resmaa Menakem writes, "Trauma is not destiny. It can be healed." To move toward a destiny of healing, we must work through the trauma that led us to need to be healed. We are dreamers, visionaries, feisty and fierce souls destined to vision something much more expansive than the conditions in place that keep us in a state of not feeling whole or seeing others as fully human or whole. We are the designers of this moment and the future; we can engage our ancestors and the knowledge that our souls are everlasting as we innovate a reality vested in our collective liberation now and into the future.

For many of us, it is difficult to trace back deep into our origins and ancestry because stories have remained untold or been buried or forgotten. Some of us do not have the resources to find out more about our genealogy or ancestry. Some of us do not want to find out more. For people who have a lineage that was fractured because of systems such as white supremacy, it can be difficult to trace back and map where we come from. For these reasons, I offer some journaling prompts followed by some guiding practices you can engage in to better understand where you are from.

JOURNALING PROMPTS

- Where do you come from? What country, landscape, surname?
- What smells, sounds, sights, and tastes were part of your origin story and the origin of those in your bloodline?
- What messages did you receive while growing up about lineage, traditions, customs, language, and cultural practices?
- Where did you learn certain values and beliefs?
- What did you know when you came into this incarnation of who you are?
- What were you told not to believe or do?
- What did you believe and do in spite of socialization and your cultural conditioning?
- What memories do you have from your childhood, neighborhood, community, faith-based spaces, and the like?

Record your answers and then ask the question again.
- Where do I come from?

STORYTELLING

Throughout the process of writing my first book, *Skill in Action: Radicalizing Your Yoga Practice to Create a Just World,* I pondered my birth story. I couldn't remember all the details and I finally decided to ask my mother to tell me about it. It became a central part of the book because of my birth story's connection to my understanding that dominant culture is designed to take the breath away from those less proximal to power. As I wrote chapter 3 of my second book, *Finding Refuge: Heart Work for Healing Collective Grief,* about my father, I asked my mother for more details about him—which branch of the military he was in, what years he served, and what her understanding was of what happened to him that made him leave the service. As I wrote this chapter about Angie, I asked my mother to share details about her with me, things I wouldn't have known.

These stories about my ancestors and my own birth story would have been lost had I not asked my mother about them. Who can you ask to share more with you about where you come from? What do you want to know about those living ancestors in your bloodline and where they come from? You might ask people you are related to by blood, or you might ask people your ancestors knew. You could even do some research through the internet, old records, and files. If none of these options seem feasible, ask for the support of Spirit, your guides, and healthy or well ancestors to share more information and stories with you about your ancestry—stories that will be supportive and helpful to you in understanding more about yourself and your relationship with others.

NOTICE

You embody all the stories, narratives, experiences, and memories of your ancestors. Notice your patterns and the people and the things you are drawn to. Notice the music you love to listen to and the foods you enjoy eating. Notice how you move in your body, what blocks there are to your movements, and where ease exists within your body. Notice your voice and hear the resonance of your ancestors in it. Notice your aversions and the things you love. Since you are made manifest because of your ancestors, the entirety of who you are and how you show up in the world is a map for understanding more about where you come from. Observe and record your observations even if you cannot explain where certain traits you embody come from or do not know the names of your ancestors. Noticing is about feeling and sensing, not overthinking.

BE GENTLE

Once you crack the doorway to understanding more about where you come from and your lineage, the doorway can swoosh open and you might find yourself in a room full of questions and feelings. Engaging with ancestors to understand more about ourselves isn't easy work. Be gentle with yourself as you learn, notice, and open up more. Take breaks when you need to, and most importantly, breathe.

When we are alone, we carry our ancestry with us. When we come together with others, we are not only bringing ourselves but also our blood memories and family histories. Even when we don't acknowledge where we are from, where we are from is always with us and present in our interactions with others. We can work with the question of where we come from and harness our ancestral energies, archetypes, and forces to support us in healing collectively. Engaging our own ancestors in private rituals and practice can be complicated. Creating healing space with others where our ancestors, different lineages, and backgrounds mingle and become actively intertwined is even more complex. If you seek to deepen your connection with your ancestors and harness their energy to support your healing process or collective healing, there are some things to consider.

Neutrality

When we come into sacred space together, we do not neutralize our identities even if we are working toward more deeply recognizing our oneness. In some spaces where rituals are practiced, there is an air of spiritual bypassing present, which can make a space for ritual go from feeling sacred to unsafe very quickly. We bring our full selves into community when we come together with others. As you come into community with others or lead rituals focused on ancestry with others, remember that rituals are not meant to erase history. They are meant to support us in being with the truth while we discern how we want to contribute to the collective healing of each other and the planet.

Power and Social Location

As you come into community with others to engage in a ritual, please be aware of your social location and power dynamics that may be present in the space due to systems of superiority and oppression. Remember, we cannot neutralize power even in a ritual or sacred space. It is present. If you happen to be leading a ritual or bringing folks together in community, please remember to acknowledge your social location as the space holder. Years ago, I cotaught an antiracism yoga class with my friend and comrade, Patty Adams. Patty and I offered this class in the wake of several Black and Brown folks being murdered by police. We had cofacilitated multiracial spaces before, and it was part of our practice to speak about our different racial identities—my Blackness, and Patty's white-bodiedness. For this particular class, we had a racially mixed group but predominantly white.

We began the class with each of us giving a dharma talk and sharing from our own experience about how we were showing up differently due to our different racial identities. We moved on to guiding people through a meditation and movement practice. During the movement practice, and as I was guiding, there was a Black person in the front row who broke down in tears at one point. This didn't feel unexpected to me because of the trauma that is housed in Black bodies from ancestors forcibly being brought to this country, the growing accounts of police brutality against Black bodies, and the anticipation of more racial trauma. I asked the group to breathe and move with the person who was now sobbing on the floor, and I went up to them to see if they needed anything from me.

We weren't in the space to explicitly talk about ancestry, but given the times in which we were living—which mirror the times we are living in now—and the racially mixed space, history, and ancestry, systemic power and oppression were alive in the room. Because of systems such as white supremacy, the trauma and gravity of that moment were landing in participants' bodies differently based on their social location and how proximal they were to power. The trauma for the Black person was expressed through wailing and sobbing, and the white-bodied people witnessed this, some with an awareness that their whiteness created the conditions that contributed to the deep grief being expressed by the Black person in our class. If you set up the container or space for ritual and practice by sharing about power and how it is present and how it might show up, and if you model this through sharing your social location, this can support the group in preparing to be in ritual together, and it can support the group in being considerate of the different social locations represented in the room.

Resilience

The purpose of knowing where we come from, coming together in community, and engaging in rituals with others using our history and ancestry as a guide is for us to multiply our collective resilience. I once heard an interview where resilience was described as not the backbone of the body or the act of standing or sitting tall but rather the muscles that support the backbone. This struck me because the muscles around the backbone keep it in place and allow the spine to support us as we stand or sit tall.

Some people resist investigating their lineage and history because of the horrors inherent in it, while others rely on their lineage to remind them of the shoulders they stand upon and the resilience embodied within them. I believe all our lineages embody resilience. We may have to dig deep for it, or simply believe it is there somewhere way back in our bloodline or much closer to our generation. My friend Marisol Jiménez McGee, a facilitator, consultant, orator, and brilliant space holder, shared the following with me during an interview about grief and liberation as part of the Healing in Community summit. She was talking about how we bond through our trauma and the importance of creating other bonds with one another.

We need bonds of light and love and wellness as much as we can, even if it doesn't fully manifest in this lifetime. Michelle, at least we're encoding it in our DNA for the next generations because our ancestors did—they taught us song and humming and art and dance and mutual aid. That's why the impulse is there. These are not new things. These are ancestral rememberings. This is what we do to survive.

In an interview I did with the psychotherapist and soul activist Francis Weller, he shared a beautiful ritual with me. In his work with the West African writer Malidoma Patrice Somé, he learned about a ritual that took place in Malidoma's village and the belief that

> We came here to give bundles away. . . . When a woman is pregnant, the shamans would come and put her into trance state so they could talk to the soul that's coming in, and they would ask, what are you bringing for us? What gifts are you bringing? And then their name would be a reflection of that medicine that is so gorgeous. Every time your name is mentioned, you're reminded you are a gift and that you're needed and necessary.[2]

Given that we all have bundles to give away, what do we want to encode in our DNA now for future generations? Not only the memories of our trauma but also the work we put into reimagining a different future and way of being. What if we came together for a ritual focused on our collective resilience—a ritual focused on yoking our lineages to heighten our ability to respond to systems of oppression and superiority that are designed for some of us to shrink while others build an inflated sense of self, often distant from their connection with other beings? What about a ritual focused on where we come from and how we want to be because "trauma isn't our destiny"? What if we came together in space for a ritual focused on our collective strength instead of how fractured we have been and may feel at this time? The following ritual is designed for a group to come together to do just that: build our collective strength.

As my friend Adriana Adelé said when talking about her ancestors,

> There are so many ways to move in a way that offers a legacy of what you want to offer and shape, not to force or impose your will but to understand this moment is made up of what has always been and creating the space for what is yet to be.[3]

PRACTICE
Our Collective Resilience Ritual

The following practices, are designed to honor the collective trauma we have experienced and our collective resilience. Journaling prompts are integrated into the practices.

INDIVIDUAL PRACTICE

This ritual involves a few steps. Please know you can practice whatever parts of the ritual that resonate most deeply with you. This ritual can be performed outside or inside.

I suggest you gather the following for this ritual:

A black candle
A white candle
A red candle
A small bowl of water
Something from the natural world that represents vitality
    and life, or a house plant.

Set up your altar space with the candles, water, and item from the natural world.

Sit in front of your altar and take some time to settle into your space. Take some deep breaths.

Light the black candle.

Light the white candle.

JOURNAL OR REFLECT ON THE FOLLOWING QUESTIONS

If I hold trauma in my body from my lineage, where is it held and how does it feel?

After you complete your journaling and reflection, take some deep breaths and record any sensations or noticings.

How is unresolved trauma showing up in the collective body?

After you complete your journaling and reflection, take some deep breaths and record any sensations or noticings.

Now I invite you to move through a progressive muscle relaxation where you will slowly tense certain parts of your body and then release them. For example, you can begin with your toes. Scrunch up your toes and release with the exhale to relax your toes. You can move on to your feet, ankles, calves, knees, thighs, and entire right leg, entire left leg, both legs. Move on to tighten and release your buttocks, hips, pelvis, low belly, low back, middle back, ribs, upper back, and chest. Move on to your hands, beginning with your fingers. Make fists with your hands and then release. Move on to your lower arms, upper arms, entire right arm, entire left arm, both arms. Last, furrow your brow and face, and release. You can stay with the progressive muscle relaxation for as long as you would like.

As you move out of the progressive muscle relaxation, reflect on the following question:

In what ways is my embodied resilience connected to that of my ancestors?

Light the red candle, which represents your bloodline.

Now take seven deep breaths.

Blow out the candles, pour the water onto the earth, and place the item from the natural world back outside.

IF YOU ARE COMING INTO COMMUNITY WITH OTHERS

You might decide to move through the individual ritual and share your experience of it with someone. If you are interested in exploring lineage and ancestry and engaging energy from your ancestors for the collective good of us all, you might begin by asking, "Where do I come from?" You can journal or create art focused on this theme. As you create, consider both the traumas and resilience contained in your lineage. You can either do this activity with someone else or share what comes through with someone in your life. As you are in community with others, consider how lineage has affected them and the space you are in with them or the relationship you have with them.

IF YOU ARE LEADING THIS RITUAL IN A GROUP

This ritual is intended to be offered in a group setting. If this is a new group and there has been no mention of power, social location, privilege, and oppression, please share the "Shared Language" and "Assumptions" sections of *We Heal Together* with participants prior to gathering together. This ritual is not intended to bypass how we may actively be contributing to another's oppression because of the identities we embody. It is a ritual that is designed to honor the collective trauma we have experienced and to honor our collective resilience.

As the facilitator of this ritual, you will need the following:

A black candle
A white candle
A red candle
A small bowl of water
A long piece of paper

Markers, colored pencils, and other art supplies to be used to
decorate the paper

Something from the natural world that represents vitality
and life, or a house plant.

This ritual can be performed outside or inside.

Set up your altar space with the candles, water, and item from the natural world, then gather the group in a circle around your altar.

The participants will need a journal and something to write with, along with anything else that might make them feel comfortable or that feels important to have in the space with them.

Begin with a moment of silence to allow people to settle into the space. After the time of silence and settling, invite people to introduce themselves to the group: name, pronouns, land acknowledgment (an acknowledgment of the indigenous land on which you are gathering), and one thing about where they come from. If you have a large group, you can have them break into small groups to do introductions. If you have a small group, have each person in the circle introduce themselves—or in some other way, until you have heard from everyone.

Light the black candle.

Light the white candle.

Now invite people to journal about the following:

If I hold trauma in my body from my lineage, where is it held and how does it feel?

After they complete their journaling and reflection, invite people to take deep breaths and to record any sensations or noticings.

How is unresolved trauma showing up in the collective body?

After they complete their journaling and reflection, invite people to take deep breaths and to record any sensations or noticings.

Now invite people to move through a progressive muscle relaxation where they will slowly tense certain parts of their bodies and then release them. For example, you can begin with the toes. Have people scrunch up their toes and release with the exhale to relax their toes. You can move on to the feet, ankles, calves, knees, thighs, and entire right leg, entire left leg, both legs. Now invite people to tighten and release their buttocks, hips, pelvis, low belly, low back, middle back, ribs, upper back, and chest. Move on to the hands, beginning with the fingers. Instruct them to make fists with their hands and then release. Move on to the lower arms, upper arms, entire right arm, entire left arm, both arms. Last, have people furrow their brow and face, and release. Invite participants to stay here for at least ten minutes resting.

As you prepare to invite participants to move out of the restful space, invite them to consider the following question:

In what ways is my embodied resilience connected to that of my ancestors?

As participants move out of the progressive muscle relaxation and rest, invite them to journal in response to the question about embodied resilience.

Light the red candle, which represents our bloodline.

Invite participants to come back together in circle and to breathe seven collective breaths.

Ask the group to feel the collective resilience in the space and envision what is possible given our collective resilience. As the group feels into their collective resilience and builds energy together through breath and presence, ask them to consider what is possible for us to create for the collective good. Once they have envisioned what is possible, roll out the long piece of paper and invite folks to draw, write a word, or use the art supplies in other ways to share what they envisioned as they tapped into the group's collective resilience. Allow time for each person who wants to participate to add to the art piece representing collective resilience.

Then invite participants to walk or move around the art piece to take in what the group has cocreated.

Close the circle by guiding participants through seven cycles of breath for seven generations in the past and future.

Blow out the candles, pour the water onto the earth, and place the item from the natural world back outside.

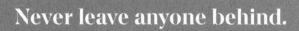

Never leave anyone behind.

—CYNTHIA BROWN

HONORING 5 EACH OTHER

It was November 13, 2016, a little less than a week after the election of Donald Trump, and I was leading my Skill in Action Yoga Teacher Training. We were sitting close in a circle with candles lit, listening to an interview with Patrisse Cullors, co-founder of the Black Lives Matter movement. Patrisse spoke about how dominant culture works to limit our imaginations and only allows us to center the experience of Black death instead of the experience of Black people living and thriving.

> Black Lives Matter is a rehumanizing project. We've lived in a place that has literally allowed us to believe and center only Black death. We've forgotten how to imagine Black life. Literally, whole human beings have been rendered to die prematurely, rendered to be sick, and we've allowed for that. Our imagination has only allowed us to understand Black people as a dying people. We have to change that. That's our collective imagination. Someone imagined handcuffs; someone imagined guns; someone imagined a jail cell. Well, how do we imagine something different that actually centers Black people, that sees them in the future? Let's imagine something different.[1]

As we listened to Patrisse, my dear friend Cynthia Brown kept coming into my spirit. Eventually, her presence felt so strong that I called her name into the circle and spoke about how she was one of the people who always imagined something different for those of us who are Black and really for all of humanity. She also and encouraged others to do the same. After the teacher training, I went to teach in a yoga studio and hold healing space for a community that felt rocked by the election of Donald Trump. Upon leaving the yoga studio, I got into my car and was met with a message on my phone from my beloved friend, Tema Okun, saying, "Cynthia is transitioning." I called Tema to ask if I should come to the hospital; of course, Tema couldn't answer this question for me. I was bone-tired and wanted to be there with Cynthia to see her and say goodbye. While I was driving home, trying to decide what to do, my nervous system took over and instructed me to go home, build an altar for Cynthia, chant, pray, and sit vigil while waiting for Cynthia to transition from her body.

I first heard about Cynthia years prior to meeting her. She was well known as a community organizer, not just in Durham—where she lived until she transitioned, but all over the state of North Carolina. I met her when I was in Tema's home one day for a meeting of our training collective, Dismantling Racism Works, dRWorks. Cynthia and Tema had been friends for years, and we wanted Cynthia to join our training group. She came into the space and I was starstruck. I had the feeling that one has when they meet someone who they have heard so much about, like a famous person. Cynthia was indeed famous. She gave me a big hug, and we sat down at the table and moved through our agenda, which was focused on allowing potential new trainers to our collective to ask questions and talk about how we might work together. After our first meeting, we met many times after that, organizing, planning, and reimagining the world in which we wanted to live.

Cynthia and I worked together for many years as colleagues and comrades. Her energy was contagious, and her smile would automatically make others smile. She was everyone's best friend and welcomed people into her life with warmth, care, and generosity. She was funny, a good cook, and her laugh would always make me summon laughter even if I didn't feel like laughing. At the end of our facilitations, Cynthia always knew what to do when we were unsure of how to close the space; she would break out in song and invite the group to sing along with her. She was honest. She would simply tell people the truth about how they were showing up in a particular space or moment. She would do this with care and compassion. She taught me so much about what it means to show up for community, center joy in my social-change work, and extend compassion, love, and grace to people who may not share the same opinion or belief system as I have. While Cynthia was clear about her values and beliefs, and convicted about creating justice in the world, she really believed in "calling in" and "calling out people" before these terms ever became part of mainstream culture. She didn't think leaving people behind was the way forward. It wasn't part of the reimagining process she wanted us all to engage in to make the world a better place.

As a supermoon lit up the sky in the early morning hours of November 14, 2016, I received a text that Cynthia had passed. The moon was closer to the earth than it had been in seventy years, and it was no surprise to me Cynthia passed on a full, super moon—her spirit matched the size of the supermoon. While I wasn't with Cynthia in person as she was transitioning, seven women were. They prepared her to transition—bathing her, placing oil on her skin, rubbing her head, holding her hand, and listening to the words of wisdom she gifted us as she was close to leaving her body: "Never leave anyone behind."

Cynthia was a community organizer at heart and knew we would need everyone involved in responding to the onslaught of trauma during the era of Trump. She knew we would need everyone to reach for hope amid despair. Cynthia could sense and see the polarization and fissures that were about to turn into gaping holes that would make it seem as if creating conditions for repair was an impossible task. In her heart and spirit, she knew we couldn't afford to leave anyone behind and that our faith would be tested in many ways as we entered into an intensely challenging time in our history.

Although Cynthia was Christian, not Buddhist, in so many ways, she embodied the spirit of a bodhisattva—an enlightened being who was most certainly on earth to help others attain their enlightenment. She knew what would happen the moment we as a collective forgot that our hearts are connected by our heartbeats and our shared history. She understood that to leave any of us behind would leave us all behind. She knew if we didn't remember our oneness with all beings, we would continue to be on a path of disconnection and strife.

Since Cynthia's passing, I've called in the words "Never leave anyone behind" in many trainings, facilitations, ceremonies, and circles. I've called her name and spirit into spaces while sharing about love—actionable love; the kind of love that is messy and real. The kind of love that is about being honest and telling the truth about how someone is showing up and how their behavior is affecting others; the kind of love that is based on the principles of transformative and healing justice. Actionable love is derived from the desire for us all to be free. To truly be committed to not leaving anyone behind means we believe people can change. We believe people can evolve and grow. We remember there was a time when we didn't know what we now know. We believe people are bigger than who they are showing themselves to be. Cynthia's wisdom wasn't about dragging people along but rather the value of not wanting to leave anyone behind, which is what systems of oppression were designed to do—leave so many of us behind.

CANCEL CULTURE

We are living during an era of cancel culture, calling people out and in, and calling on people. Cancel culture isn't a new practice or term. Still, with social media presenting a quick way to cancel people, corporations, and ideas with a single hashtag, questions about the practice of canceling someone or something have come to the forefront. I myself remember a time when I would say things like "They are not in my world." This was my coping mechanism when I wanted to block someone out of my consciousness or psyche, sometimes when they were sitting right in front of me. For me, it was usually specific to a situation, and the act of putting someone out of my world was time-limited. For example, when I planned my best friend Amy's wedding, I knew her stepmother would be a bear for us to deal with at the ceremony. She was notoriously known for being high-strung, controlling, and chaotic. She is a textbook description of a narcissist.

To focus on what I had to do, I put Amy's stepmother out of my world so she didn't distract me to lose sight of the joyous day and the tasks I had to complete to make Amy's wedding seamless. I didn't want to erase Amy's stepmother's existence, but I wanted to put her out of my mind, and for good reason. While this made sense to me at the time, by putting her out of my world, I didn't consider how she was feeling about the day or how her mental health issues were getting in the way of her being able to settle into the day; I just wanted her to disappear for a little while, and I did a good job of metaphorically making this happen. Of course, this scenario is different from systems of oppression designed to marginalize people, systematically harm entire groups of people, and not account for the harm they have caused. Still, I am left with the question of when and if canceling someone is okay. I am uneasy with the tactic of shaming others as we cancel them. I feel apprehensive about the need to take people down. Is this the way we achieve collective liberation?

In "unthinkable thoughts: call-out culture in the age of covid-19," adrienne maree brown writes,

> we've always known lynch mobs are a master's tool. meaning: moving as an angry mob, sparked by fear (often unfounded or misguided) with the power to issue instant judgment and instant punishment. these are master's tools.

we in movements for justice didn't create lynch mobs. we didn't create witch trials. we didn't create this punitive system of justice. we didn't create the state, we didn't choose to be socialized within it. we want to dismantle these systems of mass harm, and i know that most of us have no intention of ever mimicking state processes of navigating justice.

the master's tools feel good to use, groove in the hand easily from repeated use and training. but they are often blunt and senseless. unless we have a true analysis of abolition and dismantling systems of oppression, we will not realize what's in our hands, we will never put the master's tools down and figure out what *our* tools are and can be.[2]

adrienne's wisdom about how we want to move forward if we believe in dismantling systems of oppression is resonant of the wisdom the writer and activist Audre Lorde offered long ago: "The master's tools will never dismantle the master's house."[3]

What I have seen on social media is the cancelation of people's humanity. Entire campaigns to take down people—a dismissal of an individual who someone or a group of people doesn't think is "woke" enough or doing the work in the way they think someone should. I have seen the vilest comments in response to people's posts on social media. All these things have left me sitting with the quandary about how we can create change for the collective good and conditions for liberation while using tactics that dehumanize others. Can we create change and get free while simultaneously dehumanizing others? I don't think we can.

We might employ cancel culture by divesting from certain businesses because of how they treat their workers or if they only contribute to building wealth for the 1 percent. We might cancel an organization that has been repeatedly called out or in and has no interest in changing. What this feels like to me is making conscious choices that advance our movements for social change. These aren't senseless acts; they are intentional choices. When we shame people and use the same tools that have been used against so many of us who have been marginalized, I believe this moves us away from our humanity. It distracts our eyes from the prize—our collective liberation—because we are engaging in behavior that, at its core, is about dehumanization.

Cancel culture often occurs in response to having felt invisibilized. I understand wanting to engage in cancel culture, especially when all I have to do is block, restrict, report, slide into someone's social media messages, or publicly cancel someone on my own social media. I understand that systems that repeatedly oppress us through policies, practices, and cultural norms may deserve to be canceled, but what I really think many of us are calling for is for them to account for the horrid actions in which they have engaged. I think what we seek is for our hurt to be seen and responded to. I believe what we really want is for these systems that separate us from our shared humanity to stop hurting us. We seek accountability and for whoever we have decided to cancel to do something different—to change their behavior and actions and to do what is just and right.

CALLING OUT

"I'm going to call them out" is a phrase I've heard for over twenty years—maybe longer. In the past, pre-social media days, I heard it in meeting sidebar conversations, vent sessions after organizational meetings, organizing circles, conversations with family, and in many other places. In my experience, in almost all the settings in which I've seen call-out culture at play, it would often come from the recognition that harm had happened and someone having the courage to speak up and name the harm and the person or people who enacted it. I have called out many people or called out what everyone saw but no one had the will or courage to speak up about.

At times, people don't speak up because the risk may be too great, and we may want or need to maintain our role, status, and position. Due to our embodied identities and how proximal we are to institutional and cultural power, we don't all carry the same level of risk when we call out people or speak up about harm. Calling out may happen alongside canceling someone because a person is often canceled after someone has called them out on their oppressive behavior and they are unwilling to change their behavior or offer reparations to those who have been harmed.

I have witnessed calling out someone or someone's behavior as an opportunity for transformation and an invitation for repair to happen. I attended a training focused on racism, healing, and trauma several years ago. A friend convinced me to attend this training when I was preparing to move to Portland. It was the last thing I wanted to attend because I had so many tasks to tend to prior to making a cross-country move.

On day three of the training, I was sitting in the back of the circle, and the facilitators were in the front of the room. I do not remember what the focus of our discussion was, but I do remember a white woman standing up, while everyone else was sitting down. She was moving about the circle and performing her whiteness. I do not remember the words she spoke, but I do remember her body language and how her ego seemed bigger than her body. The content of what she said to the group showed she lacked awareness of her whiteness, social location in the training and world, and her impact on others—in particular BIPOC, who were less proximal to power inside and outside of the training. She had no idea she was exhibiting wanting to bypass her white privilege, even after we had spent three days talking about the history of the race construct and the trauma that manifests from white supremacy.

I watched the group respond to her with a resounding sea of "Ouches" because this is how we had decided to let someone know that harm had occurred in the space. When "Ouch" was spoken, if the perpetrator of the harm knew they had violated an agreement or made a mistake and caused harm, they were to say "Oops," and as a group, we would figure out a way to move forward. The white woman who was taking up too much space and unaware of the harm she was causing seemed shocked when she heard "Ouch," and she never said "Oops." It was at this moment that I realized why I was meant to be in that space.

The facilitators in the front of the room seemed a little frazzled and unsure of how to offer a coordinated response to the white woman and the group because no one had expected a white woman to show up so egregiously during the training. Their response was to ask the white woman to sit down and move forward with the training. I could feel the energy and anger from some of the BIPOC and white people in the group. I knew we couldn't move forward unless we addressed the "Ouches" and the lack of an "Oops" from the white woman who perpetrated harm.

I piped up from the back of the circle and said, "Can we tell her what she did so she knows and doesn't do it again?" I went on to say, "I love her enough to tell her what she did." This was my way of calling her out and acknowledging she had done something that hurt many people in the group, and it was my way of showing that we had spent three days together, we were in a group, and we could practice creating healing in the space by telling the white woman what she did and inviting her into a practice of deep exploration of her whiteness and a journey to transform her behavior in the future.

I'm not sure what allowed me to respond to her in the way I did, except that I wasn't one of the people who felt harmed. Sure, she said something that was harmful to all BIPOC people, but I didn't feel triggered by it because her behavior was almost too perfect an illustration of internalized white superiority, and I had seen that behavior several times in the past and in many Dismantling Racism and other facilitations.

At times, the process of calling out someone can begin to create repair because dominant culture thrives on a lack of transparency. It doesn't want us to be transparent about how we have been deeply conditioned by it or to speak to this conditioning when someone brings our awareness to it. Many people simply move through the world unaware of their internalized superiority due to the identities they embody that are assigned advantage and privilege until someone brings it to their awareness. This isn't an excuse; there are countless resources now about privilege and how it shows up, but we are all socialized by culture and institutions in ways that we do not always understand and are not always aware of. We must constantly work on understanding how we have been socialized and conditioned by dominant culture, and we must be vigilant about and committed to changing our behavior. This is an ongoing process.

The white woman from the training showed up in a Race & Resilience training several months later and then showed up again at another.[4] Race and Resilience is a training partnership between myself and Kerri Kelly, author of *American Detox: The Myth of Wellness and How We Can Truly Heal*. We offer trainings, workshops, and immersions focused on cultivating skills to work more effectively across lines of difference, specifically racial lines of difference. When the woman came to the Race and Resilience training, she shared, without taking up too much space, about her reflection on her behavior during the initial training where she and I first met, and she acknowledged she had work to do—a lot of work to do. This didn't erase her previous behavior, but it did make clear that she knew she needed to work on herself to better understand her privilege and how it showed up in an embodied way in order to mitigate future harm.

CALLING IN

The activist and academic Loretta Ross defines calling in as "seeking accountability from others with love and respect instead of anger and punishment. This is a learned practice and can be accomplished using various techniques. Calling in is done with love, recognizing that we're all human beings on a fragile planet and that we are all at times acting from our pain or ignorance."[5]

Calling out can be similar to calling in depending on the context and circumstances. When I stopped the group and asked if we could tell the white woman what she did, I was inviting the group to share about the impact of the white woman's harmful behavior on them. When I acknowledged loving the white woman enough to want to let her know how she harmed others with the hope she wouldn't cause harm again, I was practicing something akin to calling her in. I was seeking accountability in the group, and I was not sure the white woman had the skills or knowledge to respond to my call. I recognized her humanity while also remembering I have caused and continue to cause harm in many spaces because of what I do not know and cannot see due to my privilege and where I am assigned and given advantage because of the ways in which I have been socialized and conditioned by dominant culture like us all.

I wasn't in deep relationship with this white woman, but we were in a shared experience together, in a space of addressing why and how white supremacy causes suffering. I wasn't feeling triggered at that moment. I was feeling centered enough and healed enough to respond. Healing isn't a linear process, and I could very well lack the skill of calling in someone in the future depending on the context and nature of the harm.

Calling out can occur without a relationship other than the ways we are all interconnected. Calling in most often occurs when we have some sort of relationship with a person and are able to tell them about their missteps because of our relationship with them. A culture of care is inherent in the practice of calling in; we share because we care about the person and the people they have harmed.

The practice of calling in also suggests that whatever relationship we might have with someone who has caused harm can hold us in being honest and telling them how they are showing up. The antithesis to a call-in culture is a culture of politeness, which lacks care and honesty and so many times maintains the status quo. The practice of calling in happens most effectively when the space, organization, group, or organizing circle is a solid enough container to acknowlede harm when it happens and move through and to the other side of harm to a place of healing. Call-in culture asks for accountability and makes room for a process of repair to take place, which is impossible if we dehumanize others through canceling them.

Loretta offers wisdom about the inner work we must do to be able to call in people and the self-assessment that must take place before we do:

> Calling in begins with self-assessment. We must decide if we're in a sufficiently healed space to offer grace and forgiveness. If in a wounded space, it's okay to not take on the act of calling in and instead focus on personal healing. We must begin our calling in from a place of self-forgiveness, because it is from this self-forgiveness that we learn to extend healing forgiveness to others. Calling in also requires giving people the benefit of the doubt that they're not racist, sexist, or transphobic at their core. Calling in is not a magical power, and we cannot assume that anything will magically happen by engaging in this practice. We are only in control of our own offer of grace and forgiveness— we cannot control whether the other party accepts our offer, and we cannot take their refusal personally.[6]

The wisdom to heed is that we must do our own inner work to develop the skill of calling in, and that when we can call in someone, it is up to them to decide whether or not they will respond to our extension of grace and care with humility and a willingness to change.

CALLING ON

Calling on is a newer term used to describe an old practice and strategy: when we disrupt behavior by saying things like "I beg your pardon" or "Can you repeat what you just said?" to someone who has said something harmful. I have called on people many times by inviting them to pause, repeat what they previously said in order to hear it again, and then perhaps listen for the impact of it. Those of us who have multiple points of oppression and are engaging in our own healing work versus expending energy on calling people out or in, may decide we want to call on people because it can take less emotional labor. It requires less energy because we aren't going into a full process of calling in and creating conditions for accountability and repair to occur. We are simply disrupting the moment in a way that might allow someone to reflect on their behavior. Calling on someone doesn't require us to stay in a transformative process with someone, although transformation can happen through the process of calling on someone.

ACCOUNTABILITY

Many years ago, I sat down with my colleagues Vivette Jeffries-Logan and Tema Okun to talk about accountability. This conversation turned into an article, "Accountability in a Time of Justice."[7] During our conversations and exploration of accountability, we outlined four factors that must be in place for accountability to be built: (1) a lens through which we see these constructs of personal and institutional power, (2) an awareness that accountability is a practice of solidarity and requires us to understand our cultural conditioning and socialization, (3) a set of values or principles that serve as an anchor and place to return to as we build systems of accountability, and (4) a responsibility to take action.

We must understand that many of the identities we embody were constructed for social and political reasons. These identities, such as race, are rooted in hierarchies that were created centuries ago by white men of property. Race has no real scientific or biological basis, but it very clearly has real power that affects every part of our lives and culture. We all operate from a particular perspective based on how we've been socialized and conditioned as well as our embodied identities, those that are more proximal to power and those with less proximity to power. As we work to build systems of accountability, everyone involved must be aware of their social location and the social locations of others. Understanding our social location and positionality comes from a process of consciousness-raising, self-awareness, and awareness of the cultural context. When we enter into an accountability process, we must understand the cultural conditions in place, how power is playing out in culture, and how the cultural context and power may have influenced the conditions that led us to be working toward an accountability process.

At its core, accountability is a practice of solidarity. Building solidarity not only requires us to understand our lens, perspective, and deep conditioning but also to center relationship and authenticity. In our article about accountability, we explore how our points of privilege and oppression affect our different needs and desires for accountability: "As we negotiate our socializations, we communicate differently, bring different needs, life experiences, and stakes in our relationships based on which identity point we are moving from or most connected to in any given moment. We also hold very different desires for accountability. Therefore we must develop a level of self-awareness about our own socialization and how it inhibits or supports attitudes and behaviors that serve us and our relationships with others."[8]

We must be aware of our relationship with others due to our points of privilege and oppression, and we must work to understand how our identities might influence how we show up in relation to others, particularly if we have more power due to our social location. My desire for racism to end is based on my lived experience of being on the receiving end of white supremacy and racism. It is also based on an understanding that if I am not free, none of us are free. I desire a world free of oppression so we can all move with ease in our lives. The white-bodied people I am in deep relationship with, who are working alongside and in solidarity with me to dismantle white supremacy, may want to disrupt racism because they know it is toxic and harming Black, Indigenous, and People of Color they love.

My life and ability to thrive depends on the system of white supremacy being dismantled. White-bodied people's lives do not depend on white supremacy being disrupted or dismantled because they are benefiting from the system of white supremacy economically, socially, psychically, and physically. This positions us very differently when I call for white-bodied people to account for their participation in white supremacy. When I am engaging in an accountability process across racial difference with white-bodied people, and the principle of solidarity is being centered, white-bodied people must take the lead from me and listen to what I believe is required for them to truly be accountable.

As we write in "Accountability in a Time of Justice," "Without values or principles, accountability too often becomes a punitive instrument wielded for personal gain. Principles help us focus beyond our own socialized confusions. These values or principles are collectively created, grounded in the generational wisdom of elders, what we have learned from history, our experience, our understanding of the Creator and/or environment, and our desires for liberation." Dominant culture has equipped many of us with punitive responses to harm. If we center grounding principles during a process of accountability, this will mitigate more harm from happening and allow us to stay true to the intention and purpose of the accountability process and ultimately the outcome of repair and restorative or transformative justice. Principles such as centering the needs of the survivor or individual who has been harmed and holding the desire for our collective liberation, relationship, radical honesty, and transformation. Once we have collectively identified principles or values to center during an accountability process, it is important for us to consider what these look like in practice and also remember that accountability is a process and mistakes will be made along and toward our pathway of transformation.

The final factor we explored in our article was action:

The action component of accountability requires both relationship and principles grounded in a strong vision of transformative justice. We have seen how (white) people and groups attempt acts of accountability in isolation from those they are attempting to be accountable to and/or reinforce power constructs with a shallow understanding of what it means to "help."

Accountability requires some level of authentic relationship, even with those who are physically distant.[9]

It is one thing to understand the importance of accountability and the principles and values that support us in building accountability, and it is another thing to take action from a principled place with an awareness of social location. Sometimes people understand what is so terribly wrong in our world because of dominant culture but feel unable to contemplate where they have agency and how they can take action.

Accountability isn't possible if people are unwilling to take a risk and take action toward the goal of collective freedom. This action cannot be from a place of saviorism or done recklessly; it must be done in relationship with those most affected by oppression. We must build relationships with those most affected so we truly understand how they are being affected by systems such as racism, sexism, transphobia, classism, ableism, ageism, and the like. We need to listen, seek guidance, and take direction from those with less proximity to power about what right and appropriate action is as we work to create a world where we all have what we need to be and thrive.

The factors described above aid us in building systems of accountability; they take time to understand, process, and put in place. Many of us contemplating how to create justice, deepening our understanding of the intersection of our dharma and collective liberation, and working to create systems of accountability and repair are struggling to create less punitive responses to mistakes, missteps, and problematic behaviors. The principle I implore us to employ is the one Cynthia offered us during her passing: "Never leave anyone behind."

True accountability is grounded in the desire to not leave anyone behind—to not leave behind the people who have been harmed and are frequently in a position to experience harm due to dominant culture and their proximity to power, and to not leave behind the people who perpetrated the harm. Some people will choose to stay behind, and there is little we can do about this fact. If we are committed to bringing everyone along, understanding we are human and make mistakes and that there are things we do not know—being humble, and being devoted to our collective liberation—we have a better chance of moving forward as a collective.

The bodhisattva vow, a vow that asserts we are in relationship with all beings and that we should not leave anyone behind exemplifies how Cynthia lived her life. She vowed to see her connection with all beings and to create conditions for their liberation. She was not controlled by her desires nor did she let them get in the way of her engaging in her dharma, which was most certainly rooted in creating conditions for justice for all. And she devoted her life to God and Spirit, vowing to live her life as an expression of her connection to Spirit and knowing her passing would be a transition to a space where she could support us in continuing her legacy.

THE BODHISATTVA VOW

Beings are numberless, I vow to save them
Desires are inexhaustible, I vow to end them
Dharma gates are boundless, I vow to enter them
Buddha's way is unsurpassable, I vow to become it.[10]

As Cynthia was honored during her passing through seven women supporting her as she transitioned, she was inviting us to honor each other as we do the work of creating social change. She was asking us to center our shared humanity and calling for us to believe we could and can do better as a society and collective. She was saying, "I see you all, and I trust you to move the work forward." Her legacy includes many lessons and teachings; not leaving anyone behind is a teaching we desperately need during a time when systems are working every minute of every day to leave so many of us behind.

Below you will find some questions to consider based on the practice of not leaving anyone behind.

JOURNALING PROMPTS

- What conditions need to be in place for us to truly honor one another—our humanness, mistake-making, not knowing, and all the ways we cannot or do not understand how we cause harm?
- What conditions need to be in place for us to create a culture that cancels people less and centers relationship more?
- What does it mean to you to never leave anyone behind, and why is this important at this time?
- How can we move closer to our humanity by recognizing the humanity in others?

These aren't easy questions to answer, but Cynthia never said the work and practice of creating conditions for collective liberation would be easy. In fact, she said the opposite: "This *work* isn't easy, and we *have* to do it anyway."

PRACTICE

Never Leave Anyone Behind

The following practice offers guidance on dreaming of a world where we do not leave anyone behind as Cynthia so aptly invited us to do.

INDIVIDUAL PRACTICE

Take some time to reflect on your definition of accountability and what it means to you to not leave anyone behind. How would it feel? What would your life be like? How would you relate to other beings?

If you feel moved, I invite you to write a vow or commitment with accountability in mind.

For example:

I commit to seeing my connection with all beings, everywhere.
I commit to taking action in my life that will support the collective good.
I commit to devoting myself to something bigger than myself.
I commit to creating conditions for less punitive systems and instead, systems of repair.

Once you have written your prayer, please say it aloud three times, noticing what sensations and emotions arise as you do. Then commit to returning to your prayer or vow each day for a month and continue to record sensations and emotions that arise. You might even note how your feelings about the vow changes or how the vow or prayer changes you.

IF YOU ARE COMING INTO COMMUNITY

Practice the individual practice and notice how the vow or prayer shifts your relationship with others as you come into community with them. Record any noticeable changes.

IF YOU ARE LEADING A GROUP

This practice is meant to be done in a group setting—either in a meeting, community, organization, or any group of people who have come together to practice rituals based on our collective liberation such as yoga, meditation, study groups, community organizing groups, etc. This practice will work best if you are with a group of people with whom you have established a common goal or reason for coming together and some sort of agreements or guidelines.

For this practice, group participants will need their imaginations, cozy things for a deep rest practice, a sheet of paper, and something to write with.

Gather with your group and take a moment to center yourself and the group. Then review your agreements or guidelines.

For this practice, you will invite people into a deep rest and then move them out of it and ask them to reflect. You can repeat the progressive muscle relaxation in chapter 4 or use a different mindfulness and relaxation technique. People can be as cozy as they would like with blankets, pillows, sacred objects, or other things that might bring them comfort and allow them to rest. Guide them into a space of relaxation and rest, and allow them to be in silence resting for at least five minutes. After five minutes have passed, invite the group to begin dreaming of a world wherein no one was left behind. A world where systems, people, policies, and culture do not throw away people or our responsibility to the planet. Invite them to dream about what is possible and to reimagine what we have now to create a different future for ourselves and future generations. Encourage them to focus on our shared humanity and to truly dream of a world where no one is left behind, not even those who have participated in oppression. We have all been the oppressor and are implicated in systems that are meant to divide us from ourselves and one another. Dreaming requires the mind to be still and the consciousness to roam. Encourage participants to allow their minds to imagine things that may not seem possible but are because our dreams can come into being.

Allow them to dream for at least five minutes, maybe more. When you are ready to bring them out of the relaxation, do so slowly. Invite them to engage gentle movements, such as wiggling their toes and fingers or turning their head from side to side. Invite participants to rise back up into a seated position if they are not already in one. Guide the group to breathe together for seven cycles of breath; to breathe life into their dreams. Then bring them back up to the surface and into the space. Participants might want to move a little after their rest and dreaming session. Encourage them to do so and then bring everyone back together in the group.

Now invite people to write down one practice that might support us in creating the world they dreamed of—for example, remembering our interconnectedness, listening to what people need, knowing intent and impact aren't the same. Once everyone has written down their practice, invite them to walk into the middle of the circle and place their piece of paper there. After everyone has shared, invite people to view all the words in the center and have someone in the group share the words aloud.

Give people a few minutes to digest the words and experience. As you feel ready, transition the group out of the practice.

Even a wounded world is
feeding us. Even a wounded
world holds us, giving us
moments of wonder and joy. I
choose joy over despair.

—ROBIN WALL KIMMERER

MOMENTS OF JOY
AND WONDER

When I was a little girl and it was picture day at school, my mother would dress me up in something cute and send me off to pose and smile. I would go to school, wait for the office to call my class down to the room where the photographer was waiting, and sit down in whatever scene the photographer had set. I was reticent each time I sat down to be photographed, and it showed because I would never smile in my childhood school pictures.

I wasn't an unhappy child; I was a serious child. I was a Black child going to school in an almost all-white school. At times, I was aware I was treated differently than my classmates by teachers and school administrators. I was aware some of my white peers had been conditioned to believe that different races were less than as evidenced by a little boy calling me a "nigger" on the playground when I was in first grade. I knew my mother worked tirelessly as a special education teacher, while some of my peers' parents had more wealth, bigger homes, more options, more time, and hired people to clean their homes and tend their gardens—people who looked just like me and my mother: Black. I felt the sense of disconnection present in people based on how they dismissed each other and moved past each other, seemingly unaware of their humanity and connection to other beings.

I believe I didn't smile in pictures because I understood a snapshot wouldn't cover up all I was aware of. A snapshot captures a second in time but isn't representative of the whole of time nor what came before the photograph or after. When invited to smile prior to the camera's flash, I would stare right into the camera with a serious look, and the photographer would snap the photo and send me back to class. And when I would come home from picture day, my mother would ask me how it went. I would usually reply, "Fine."

We would wait until proofs arrived in the mail. Every year, when my mother received the proofs, she would look at me and ask, "Why didn't you smile?" Every year, my response was the same: "Because it was raining." She would follow up and say, "Michelle, it couldn't have been raining. The sun was out. How come it rains every time picture day rolls around?" I would assert once again that it was most definitely raining, and my mother would drop the conversation.

Even though I had chosen not to smile in the photos, my mother would pick a proof that she felt was the cutest and order a plethora of wallet-sized 4 x 6 and 8 x 10 photos. This was a ritual that felt important to my mother but not that important to me. She would share my photo with relatives and friends, mailing them out in greeting cards; and she would hang an 8 x 10 in the house. The walls of our home were covered in these 8 x 10 photos. My brother's photos always showed his smile, and mine, well, showed an honest expression of how I felt about the times we were living in year after year.

The truth is, it wasn't raining every picture day, but I felt like my internal environment was gray and rainy; the outer world and all that was happening in it affected my insides. I wasn't an unhappy child, but I was longing for a real conversation about whether other children—or adults, for that matter—noticed what I noticed. I wanted to know if other people also stood in their driveways waiting for a spaceship to take them away because the world's heaviness felt like too much. I wanted to know if the Black housekeepers and gardeners who worked for many of my white classmates' families were happy and cared for. I wanted to know why people were treated differently due to the way they looked and the identities they embodied. I wanted to know if anyone else felt as sensitive as I did.

THE WOUNDED WORLD

As a child, I felt the wounded world in my bones, and knew I wanted others to stop and notice the wounds and that I wanted to be part of healing them. I am not sure how I knew there were wounds that needed to be healed or that there were wounds covered with subpar bandages not meant to heal them. I am not sure why I felt it all so deeply, but I did. And I was curious about the wounds.

I was curious about why my mother would always say "It's too painful" when asked about our ancestors and those who were enslaved. Or why children would come up to my mother unprompted—sometimes when their parents were unaware—and hold her hand, seeing her as someone who wouldn't wound them, as a safe person. I knew wounds existed in my family when whispers of family secrets would emerge as we were eating dinner at my grandmother's table. Or when I saw my grandfather, Fred, in his TV room, drinking whiskey and hiding. As part of my mother's job as a special education teacher, she made home visits to check on her students and their families. I knew wounds were present in these homes as I witnessed families who seemed broken with children uncared for.

I was wised to the stories my teachers would tell us about the Indigenous people breaking bread with the colonizers when we visited Jamestown and Colonial Williamsburg. I knew there was more to the story and that our history books conveniently left out the more complex and honest parts of it. I knew wounds existed in the world as I watched the ramifications of the Exxon Valdez oil spill as birds were being washed off with Dawn dish soap by rescuers. I was aware of some of the world's wounds and carried my own wounds associated with lineage and history. These wounds and so many more moved with me. They shaped me. They changed how I viewed myself and the world. They ignited urgency inside me that arose from not wanting us to continue to wound one another.

As an adult, I continue to feel the wounded world in my bones and want to be part of living in the wounded world while also healing our collective wounds. The world can feel so overwhelming at times. There is too much for us to respond to, and our hearts can grow weary. Even though our hearts can break and open, again and again, the cycle can become tiresome. What I have learned over time about the wounded world is that for me to stay alive, present to my life, connected to others and the natural world, and be engaged in creating and reimagining a world where fewer wounds occur, I must build the capacity to be with the wounds. I must work to mitigate more cycles of suffering, and remember that the world's heaviness exists alongside all the joy and magic the world creates in collaboration with us. I must remember this because of what my friend and teacher Lama Rod Owens, a Buddhist minister, activist, and author, reminded me of when he spoke so eloquently in an interview on my podcast, *Finding Refuge*:

> This life is just an experience. This world is just an experience that I'm having; it is as real as everything else is real. I have to balance things—the identity of being in this body at this time with this deeply held belief that this is also an experience that I am moving through. This and this experience of being in the world in this moment. A world that is not my home. I'm not going to be here forever, but I'm also committed to alleviating the discomfort that this time in place creates for all of us, even if it's just a dream and the dream. And, you know, when you're really invested in that teaching it doesn't mean that you stop caring about the world, but the world gets a little more spacious. This is just one experience, you know, that's happening, but over time, as we practice our practice—our meditation or yoga and so forth—we, our minds begin to expand, they begin to open. We begin to have a sense of the multiple things are happening in one moment. There are multiple planes and multiple dimensions happening.[1]

There are indeed multiple experiences happening at one time and I want us all to feel more spacious and expand.

A PLACE FOR OUR JOY

Heaviness and joy can exist at the same time. Grief and joy often dance with each other. Heartbreak and joy are good companions. Being present to our wounds and healing isn't mutually exclusive. As we do the work of healing ourselves and the world, it is necessary for us to find and feel joy amid all the suffering. Joy can aid us as we come together to heal. Joy is connected to our ability to find peace even amid heaviness or hardship.

Joy is often experienced when we trust we are held by Source, ancestors, or something bigger than ourselves. Because joy is associated with peace—peace with ourselves and where we are—it is less fleeting than happiness, which is often an outward expression in response to external things such as situations, people, and events. We certainly should be able to feel happy when there is more levity in the world and less heaviness. I want to inspire us to find joy as we respond to the world's heaviness, as we work to create a better world for ourselves and future generations, and as we work to heal our own wounds and the wounds of the collective.

What I have witnessed in many people and groups is a resistance to feel and cultivate joy. Even though I felt the heaviness of the world at a young age, I know many children feel glee and joy more freely than many adults. Something happens to us through a process of conditioning, socialization, and experiencing trauma that makes us believe there is no place for joy. To me, this suggests that many of us are taught or trained to resist and deny our own joy, either because we do not think we are worthy of experiencing joy or we are taught it is wrong to feel joyful.

How we have been socialized shapes our conditioned responses, how we relate to self and others, and how we relate to emotions and experiences including joy. Many of us have been socialized to deprioritize joy and place greater value on the challenges we face in our lives because "challenges build character." We have been conditioned to believe that worthy things only come through hard work, not through allowing ourselves to feel joyful or, dare I say, free.

Some of this socialization comes from ancestral patterns and stories. For example, in my own family, I know it was difficult for my ancestors who were enslaved to find joy as they picked cotton, tended the land for plantation owners, and lived in inhumane conditions as they witnessed and experienced some of the most hideous forms of violence and oppression. But I also know they communicated in song, laughed to feel free, and made magic with the resources they had. They celebrated and felt joy around holidays, births, weddings, and their small victories toward freedom. Had they not been able to find joy as they experienced suffering, they would not have been able to face the conditions put in place for them by white supremacy.

If my mother only thought about cotton pricking her fingers as she picked it, or if my great-grandmother had only thought about not knowing her father because her family was split apart in a slave auction, or if my grandfather had only thought about how difficult it was to work on the railroad at the age of ten, they wouldn't have been able to smile, celebrate, or rejoice. Oppression would have successfully stolen their joy, and they weren't willing to have their joy taken.

While some of our conditioning may be ancestral, some of it comes from messages we receive from our families. We may have received messages about working hard and *then* playing—or not playing at all, as if there was no role for play in work or play as work. The messages I received from my own mother were about endurance and meeting challenges. I believe this came from her having to endure difficult situations and overcome challenges. These are not unhandy skills to learn. I learned how to be tenacious and persevere. The number of times I witnessed my mother deprioritize her own joy because of whatever challenges were present at the time are too many for me to count on my fingers and toes. She sacrificed her joy at times so my brother and I could feel joy, and something about this felt unbalanced to me, even as a young child. She felt the world's heaviness as well.

We are conditioned by not only our families or caretakers but also dominant culture. Because I am a Black woman, dominant culture works to steal my joy. I embody points of oppression, and oppression in its very nature is intended to smother any joy I might feel or access. White supremacy sees Black people as a people who can endure pain and furthermore, should feel pain, not joy. As a cisgender woman, sexism, patriarchy, and Christianity work to control my body and access to pleasure in the name of purity being a virtue and pleasure being a sin. Many of us who embody points of oppression and are less proximal to institutional and cultural power have been told we have no right to be joyous or make space for joy as a way of taking back our sovereignty. Capitalism works to make us consume things to gain a false sense of joy, as if buying our joy is the only way to experience it. When, in fact, it is impossible to buy joy and peace. The messages we have internalized from dominant culture—a culture that, even for those more proximal to social and institutional power, isn't about joy but instead greed and upholding systems of dominance that aren't based on joy but based on being in control and controlling others are messages to keep us joyless. They are meant to keep us in a place of suffering and intended to make us forget that we have a choice about how we relate to our suffering. The result of our socialization and dominant culture's influence makes it such that even when we might be able to access joy, we deny ourselves the experience of it.

Dominant culture would have us believe that joy isn't valuable and that we cannot create it ourselves. This is dominant culture's strategy to keep us in the cycle of continuing to uphold it. In "The Theft of White Supremacy," Kaitlin Curtice writes about the ingrained pattern of stealing in systems of supremacy and the cycle of fear that makes us continue to yield to a scarcity mindset:

Supremacy steals everyday joy from the people it targets. It steals their livelihood and their pride, sometimes their very lives. When fear takes over a body, mind, and spirit, that fear feeds the idea that to make things right again, something should be taken, and one must do whatever is necessary to get it."[2]

Kaitlin is correct. The cycle of fear keeps us trapped and believing we have to steal or take to bring things back into balance for ourselves while the world continues to be utterly imbalanced because of supremacy, unprocessed trauma, and systems of oppression. Systems of supremacy steal our joy every minute of every day and make those who are oppressing and doing the stealing believe it is bringing them joy to take from others. This is false. Stealing joy, humanity, truth, history, culture, and so forth doesn't breed joy, just more suffering.

Dominant culture doesn't want us to center joy because if we do—and if we recognize joy might bring us closer to freedom—we might begin to operate outside of the norms of systems of dominance and instead strive to create our joy and create conditions for the collective to thrive. Experiencing joy feels like a slap in the face to systems that want us to feel oppressed, suppressed, and hopeless. Many of us have been so shamed when we have centered joy in our lives. This is a tool of the master. The system that says you are undeserving of peace, happiness, or your heart feeling full. This is deeply toxic and will only lead to more toxicity.

Even in our work to create change for the betterment of the world and us all, we are taught that the work we do to create change within ourselves and others must be challenging and joyless. For those of us working in movement circles, volunteering, or organizing, there is a deep-rooted myth that we must die for the cause because this is the only way social change occurs. We must work ourselves to death to create liberation for others at the expense of our own liberation. Or our commitment to the cause is only measured in hard work. These beliefs aren't based on care, joy, or liberation. They are a way white supremacy and capitalism sustain themselves to keep us believing we must toil and tire as we do our work instead of centering joy as a vital part of social change.

As I engage in my dharma of making this world better as homage to those who came before me and those who will come after me, if I am not prioritizing my own healing, do not have the resources I need to heal, or am not engaged in a healing process and practice, how can I create a space for healing? As the feminist, healer and organizer, Omisade Burney-Scott explains,

> I do not want to show up in movement spaces, busted up and broke down. If the analogy is that we all jump in this car and we show up in this amazing green crisp cool place that's called liberation, but I can't get out of the car cause my leg is fucked up . . . I don't want that. I don't want that for myself. I don't want that for you. I don't want that for anybody . . . I want you to be able to take full advantage of this liberatory space. I want you to access it. I want you to feel it. I want you to smell it, I want you to enjoy it.[3]

If we are not caring for ourselves, which I believe includes a practice of bringing joy in our lives and work, then it will be difficult to arrive at the "amazing green crisp cool place called liberation" that Omisade dreams of.

Given that, for so many of us, there is a deeply embedded narrative that we are undeserving of joy—it's woven into our tissues and cells. We must turn toward developing practices to create, find, feel, and allow joy in our lives and movements for social change. We must turn dominant culture on its head, burn it down, disrupt it, and shake out the notion that joy is unattainable.

My friend, and a trans yoga teacher and activist, Allé K. writes about this so eloquently from their lived experience.

> Joy is inherent to our survival as humans, as marginalized people, fat trans people, especially. Joy is inherent to activism, to being change-makers in this world. We often think, or I do at least, that we have to be serious all the time, fighting the good

fight 24/7 if we want to see change ... but that's not sustainable. I learned during the summer of 2020 in the protests after the murder of George Floyd [by police]. We need rest, healing, and joy in order to be able to sustain the fight for collective liberation. We must center joy and healing in our process if we are to maintain our energy and our work.

Joy to me as a fat trans person looks like:

cooking green fried tomatoes
grilling at the pool in summer
fall drives on the parkway to see the leaves
yoga at the park on a sunny day
hugging another person, especially a fellow fat/trans
    person
laughing in public not worrying about who's looking
seeing others who've overcome obstacles, especially
    systemic oppression thrive
bathing at night with the lights off & candles lit
reading a book about a trans person by a trans person
seeing myself in main characters, represented in the
    media & arts
embodied essence be it bravery, laughter, community,
    quietude.[4]

My own journey to finding joy has been a process. It has been a practice of being able to be with the despair and heartbreak present in the world and to be able to feel sometimes fleeting and other times sustained moments of joy. I understand for you that joy may mean something different than it means to me, and I encourage you to consider your definition of joy so you can recognize it when it is present. For me, joy is deeply connected to care. If I am not caring for myself, if I am disembodied or disconnected from my life and self, then it is difficult for me to find joy. If I am not refilling my cup, I feel empty and unable to give to others.

CARING FOR OURSELVES

A healer, responsible steward of the planet and activist, Kennae Miller offers wisdom around what it means to practice care and the lessons she has learned from nature about the importance of care.

I make sure I'm checking on all of my plants around the house, whether that's touching the soil or pulling off dead leaves or just nurturing and caring for them again. My connection to nature teaches me a lot of lessons. One of my teachers challenged me to keep a plant journal of my garden and plants, and it gave me a big lesson on self-care. I noticed there was a group of my plants that looked like they were dying. They weren't brown and crispy, but they definitely looked like they were on their way to dying. When I looked at them or when I went to care for them, the first thing I did was check the water meter.

After I checked the water meter that was in the plant, then I checked another meter that I have on my refrigerator, which tells me how humid it is and what the temperature of the house is. The water heater tells you if the soil is moist and the plants are getting enough light. I thought both of these seem fine, but the plants look like they're dying still. So I went to get water. At that moment, what I heard Spirit say was the way that you're treating your plants right now, checking the meters and trusting these meters to say that it's okay is the way that you're treating yourself. You're thinking, "Okay, I drank water yesterday. I really don't need water today." Or "You had eight hours of sleep two weeks ago, so you're fine." Listening to that lesson as I was caring for the plants reminded me that I'm not gonna bloom flowers or put out new leaves by not caring for and nurturing myself in the way that I need. Soil needs to be tended to; sometimes it's too alkaline, or sometimes it's too acidic. How does that come into balance?[5]

I love this offering from Kennae because she shares the lesson of how nature is a reflection and mirror for us. It is also a teacher. When she used the meter to measure the moisture, it was indicating the plants had enough moisture but the plant was dying and did not have enough moisture. I liken this to when we tell ourselves we are okay or we've paid enough attention to ourselves or extended care, but we still feel depleted, unmotivated, or uninspired. She realized there was more to it than the meter reading and connected this with herself by sharing that it is impossible to put out new leaves or bloom if we do not tend ourselves. This led her to think more deeply about how she was caring for herself. If we are being careless about taking care of ourselves, it will be difficult to feel or find joy.

I find joy through a consistent practice of meditating, praying, and using divination tools. Joy comes to me when I am out in nature, connecting with friends, tending my garden, digging in the dirt, singing, laughing, watching the hummingbirds, and talking to the honeybees. I feel joyful when I sit still and listen to the sounds of nature and myself. I find joy in connecting with my ancestors, both living and those who have transitioned. I find joy in the circles I hold in my home as we gather to eat, drink, laugh, and journal.

My comrade Kelley Nicole Palmer says, "When I center my joy, joy pervades every single thing that I do."[6] Joy comes to me when I am around others who are able to access joy. I feel joyful as I allow myself to engage in activities that bring me pleasure. I feel most joyful when I don't feel as if I have to work for or earn my right to joy, when it unexpectedly comes to me. For someone who feels so much of the world's heaviness, I find joy in many spaces. Sometimes I have to look for it, and sometimes I have to work to remember to make space for it. I need to be able to feel joyful to continue to respond to the world's heaviness.

GUILT AND JOY

I want to offer a few words about guilt and joy. While I believe heaviness and joy can exist at the same time and grief and joy are often dance partners in our lives, I do not believe guilt and joy are the most natural of partners. Often guilt is associated with shame, and shame gets in the way of joy. As a clinical social worker for many years, I have heard countless clients share about grieving the loss of a person or dream and feeling guilty about feeling joyful during a respite from their grief. I have heard clients share they feel shame about feeling joy while so much trauma is occurring in the world. I have heard friends share their experiences of moments of joy during a time when they were also grieving, and the tension and dissonance present, causing them to wonder if are denying the loss they have experienced.

I understand these feelings. What I have come to learn is that we can experience many things at once—we do not have to feel guilty about feeling joyful even amid so much chaos and trauma in our lives and in the world. In fact, we need to feel joy and remember it is available to us and will likely visit us again in moments of despair, when we are grieving, and when we feel lost. We need to remember what brings us joy in moments when it feels as if all is lost. If you find yourself feeling guilty about experiencing joy, be kind to yourself and remember that feeling guilt or shame in a moment of joyousness could lead to more heaviness, and the world is already heavy enough.

I was leading a workshop about mindfulness in the workplace while the war in Afghanistan was ending, COVID-19 numbers were once again rising, and the overwhelm in the world was quite intense. I led the group through a few mindfulness practices and was sharing about intergenerational trauma and how trauma affects us as individuals and a collective. A man asked a question about our moral responsibility to respond to what was happening in the world. I appreciated his question; it seemed to come from a place of curiosity about how the mindfulness practices I was leading folks through might relate to disrupting the tragic things happening around us. I responded to him by saying, "We do have a moral responsibility to respond to what is happening in our world. We have little control over some of what is going on and a lot of control over other things. We have contributed to so much of the destruction, oppression, and dysfunction we are experiencing at this time." I went on to say, "We cannot solve every problem we are facing. I wish we could. It isn't humanly possible for us to respond to all the tragedies. The world is overwhelming, and at times it is this way because we make it so."

A couple of weeks after the training, I reflected on his question about our moral responsibility to disrupt what is happening in our world. I also remembered we can only do so much. We cannot take care of everyone and everything. I wish we could. I reflected on what it might be like to feel okay about what we can do and, for the collective good, to bring joy in the work we are doing to change the world in the way we know how. I thought about it not being an either-or. I can feel joy about what I am doing to change the world for the better. I can bring joy to my work, which is very much focused on changing the world. I feel like there is too much to do. I can feel sad about what is happening in the world. I cannot fix it all, and trading my joy in for working myself into the ground by trying to fix everything isn't a fair deal to me. It isn't a deal I am willing to make.

Santosha, one of the *niyamas* (moral observances) from yogic philosophy, means contentment, and practicing it is the key to finding joy and feeling joyful amid suffering. *Santosha* is about being content or rather accepting what is happening as it is. This does not absolve us of our moral responsibility to change what is happening or intervene to disrupt the unjust things happening in our world, but instead asks us to look at what is happening as it is and to work to allow joy to exist alongside the things happening in the world meant to make us or others suffer and feel joyless.

There are so many barriers to us feeling joy and finding peace, especially for those of us who are more aware of systemic barriers and the impact they have on our bodies, hearts, minds, and spirits. We must go through a learning process to understand that joy can coexist with the world's heaviness. My child self in my school pictures didn't understand this. I didn't feel at peace because I felt the world wasn't at peace and there was no room for joy. The urgency I felt about the problems I saw in the world didn't make space for joy.

I've learned to find and create joy where I can. As we come together to heal in community, it is imperative that we build the skill of being joyful and accessing peace as we heal. Finding joy is a central part of our process as we move toward healing.

The invitation to feel and connect with joy isn't encouragement to bypass what is happening in our world and what so desperately needs to change. I am asking for joy to be recognized as part of our human experience, if we allow ourselves to find, reconnect to, and feel it. I am suggesting the heaviness of the world and the suffering so many of us face is not the only experience that is happening. There is more. I am inviting us to feel into what else is present and available in our experience of being a human on earth at this time. I am inviting you into a process of discovery about joy—the messages you've received about your own right to feel joy and about others and their right to joy; the practices that bring joy to you and how you resist your own joy; how oppression and the work we do to dismantle it can be done in a way that either leaves us feeling joyless or joyful.

In the next section of this chapter, I offer journaling prompts, individual practices to connect with joy, practices that you can engage if you are curious about coming into community with others, and practices focused on joy intended to be done in organizations and social change spaces, and a ritual meant to be done in ceremony. You can adapt these practices to fit your setting and the context where you are digging your joy wellspring.

I welcome you to respond to the following journaling prompts as a way of exploring your definition and relationship to joy.

JOURNALING PROMPTS

- What is your definition of joy?
- What brings joy to you?
- What do you notice when you do not resist joy and instead embrace it?
- Are there practices you've used in the past to connect with joy when feeling despair, sadness, or overwhelm?

- What unexpected joy have you experienced today or in the last week?

PRACTICE

Finding Joy in a Wounded World

INDIVIDUAL PRACTICES

I offer a few individual practices knowing there are many. Feel free to add to this list from your own experience.

Connecting With My Relations

In my experience, in the moments when I am feeling despaired or overwhelmed by the world's heaviness, I go inward and retreat. This is a similar response to how many people respond to shame—they go inward and retreat. While retreating may be necessary for me to come back into balance, what has felt more powerful for me is to connect with others. Despair is part of our human experience, especially because we are living in a world where so much strife exists, and despair can feel limiting and constraining. Connection, to me, feels the opposite of retreating.

In previous chapters I have offered a few different ways to connect with the natural world—in groups, ceremonies, and with the elements and ancestors. Some of these connections may elicit joy, which can be such an important part of our healing process. Some of these connections may elicit other emotional responses or experiences. To find joy, I invite you to connect with those people, beings, or experiences that bring you joy. You can connect with an old friend who you know will make you laugh. You can connect with an animal companion or furry being who brings you joy and may remind you to play.

You might decide to connect with the earth by going on a walk and noticing the colors, sounds, sunlight, a water source, old tree, new bloom, or the leaves changing as the seasons do. Connect with things that delight you and remind you there are many things happening at once: despair and delight, heaviness and lightness, sadness and wonderment. At different times we need different things to reconnect to joy. You might find a nature walk brings you into a joyful and peaceful place one day, and the next day perhaps it will not be as effective. This may be the day you call an old friend who can make you laugh. Or you watch a funny movie to connect to humor. The point here is to connect. Connect with something or someone outside yourself to find joy and a sense of peace within yourself.

Joy List

When you are feeling joyful, or content and at peace, take some time to make a list of what brings you joy. This list might include people's names, places that bring joy to you, poems, or books that make you feel joyful, artistic activities that bring you joy, and more.

Move Your Body

Yesterday, a friend texted me to ask how she could get the anger out that she was feeling regarding her parents' selfishness. I texted back, "Move your body." When we move our bodies, energy moves. Things shift. I told her to run, dance, shake, or work in her orchard. I was inviting her to change her experience in order to both release her anger and come back into balance. I suggest we do these same things to find and feel joy, to reconnect and remember our natural state, which is one of contentment and joy. I am not much of a dancer but I've never felt bad after an impromptu dance party or when I've danced and no one has been watching. Get the energy flowing with movement. Be silly. Laugh at yourself and feel joyful.

Gratitude Practice

I have kept a gratitude journal since 2016. I write ten gratitude statements every day about big and small things I feel grateful for. I know at times dominant culture bypasses the despair it creates by focusing on positivity instead of truth. Gratitude statements, for me, are a way to honor what I feel grateful for even as so many things might be falling apart in the world. The practice came to me during a time of great crisis, and it did as all the research in positive psychology suggests—it made me happier, more content, and at peace.

Expressing gratitude is another way to connect to something outside myself because it prompts me to reflect on people, experiences, pets, beings in the natural world—such as the crows cawing as I write this paragraph now, and other gifts. It is a way of moving away from what I don't have, to focus on how much I do have. The brain is conditioned to focus on lack or scarcity, not on gratitude and abundance. Creating a gratitude list is a way of shifting this conditioning, and it has been a very powerful practice and tool for me. It has certainly made me feel more joyful. To take this one step further, you might let the people, experiences, pets, beings in the natural world, and so forth, know you feel grateful for them, which is a way of extending yourself even further and expressing your gratitude outwardly.

COMMUNITY PRACTICES

These practices are designed to be done in community with others. As with the individual practices, I will offer a few practices here and invite you to add to this list. Any of the individual practices listed above could be done in community with others. In addition, you could use any of the journaling prompts as an opening prompt in a meeting or gathering.

Connection in Community

The connection practice could be done in a few different ways within community. You and others could share about an unexpected joy you all experienced over the last month. You could share about why in despairing times it is important to remember what brings us into a larger sense of connection with others to learn more about the value of connection.

If you have access to the outdoors, perhaps you and others could go on a nature walk, noticing the colors, sounds, shapes, sunlight, and so forth. At a certain point in the nature walk, you could ponder what in the natural world brings joy to each of you.

Joy List

Create a list with others about what brings joy to you all. Post this list somewhere in a space where everyone can access or see it.

Move Your Bodies Together

I once worked with an organization that had an impromptu dance party at 2:30 p.m. each day. Of course, this was not everyone's cup of tea. I thought it was a creative idea. They would make an announcement over the intercom, put on music, and people could either dance in their offices or come into a common space and dance together. Of course, people weren't required to dance; sometimes people would come to be in the energy of the space and watch as their colleagues shook a leg.

Structured movement can be offered in community with others. Invite someone from outside the group to lead movement of some kind, or if this is an ongoing community group, you could rotate facilitation of movement along group members.

Ceremonial Gratitude Practice

The following practice is meant to connect us with joy as we come together with others. This practice can be completed as a ceremony in a community group, a place of faith, as part of a spiritual gathering, in an organization, or in an organizing circle.

For this practice, you will need to bring something small to the ceremony that represents sweetness and joy—for example, a rose tea bag, a dab of honey, chocolate, dates, and the like. The person convening the group or someone in the group needs to bring a candle, thick paper or durable cloth such as burlap or cotton, and a gold string.

Invite people to make a circle, place the thick paper or durable cloth in the center of the circle. Place the candle to face the south, and light the candle.

After you have lit the candle, invite people to find a comfortable way to be in their bodies, close their eyes if that is okay for them to do, and take a few deep breaths. Invite them to take a moment to breathe and arrive in the space. Once you feel as if the energy has shifted and people have moved into stillness, say the following prayer:

> May the sweetness of our circle bring us joy.
> May we know the experience of joy as our birthright.
> May joy be present in our lives.
> May we heal and know joy.
> May we bring joy to others.
> May we remove all that is in the way of us, as a
> collective, finding joy and peace.

After you have said the prayer, invite the group to take a few more deep breaths and to work with the following mantra: *May joy light the pathway to our collective healing.*

Invite group participants to repeat this five to ten times to themselves or aloud as an entire group.

After the mantra practice, invite participants to come back into the space by gently blinking open their eyes and taking a moment to reorient to the space.

Once the meditation, prayer, and mantra are completed, invite participants to reflect on a time when they experienced joy amid despair, trauma, discord, or chaos. Have them journal or meditate on this experience for five to seven minutes. As they reflect, you can play some quiet and joyful music. After they finish journaling, invite them to pair up in dyads with someone and share about their reflection. Allow about three minutes per person, for a total of six minutes per dyad. You can keep time for them.

After each person in the dyad has shared, have them take a moment to notice how they feel after having shared their experience of joy amid contrasting experiences or emotions.

Invite the dyads to now share how it felt to share about joy and how it felt to receive a story about joy.

Last, ask the dyads to discuss the role of joy in our collective healing.

Bring the group back together.

Now invite each person to bring a piece of the sweetness they brought to the ceremony into the center of the circle. They will place a portion of their sweetness on the paper or cloth and share something about it. After everyone has shared, fold the cloth, making a wrap to contain the sweetness and tie it with a gold string.

Once the packet has been tied, return to the earlier mantra: *May joy light the pathway to our collective healing.* Invite the group to say this aloud five to ten times.

Close the circle by saying the following prayer once again:

May we remember the sweetness.
May we continue to be a circle that lights the pathway
    to our collective healing.
May we know joy.
May we be joy.

As you feel moved, close the circle by moving the candle to the north side of the center of the circle and blowing it out.

As the group or ceremony convener or holder, take the packet of sweetness and offer it to the elements. You can do this by burning it and offering sweetness to the fire, or allowing it to travel down a stream or the river. You can offer it to a mighty tree or a special outdoor altar. Allow the sweetness and joy to linger and for joy to pervade, expanding out from the circle into the larger vessel of joy that allows joy to move through us and everything.

The graveyard is the richest place on earth, because it is here that you will find all the hopes and dreams that were never fulfilled, the books that were never written, the songs that were never sung, the inventions that were never shared, the cures that were never discovered, all because someone was too afraid to take that first step, keep with the problem, or determined to carry out their dream.

—LES BROWN

7

DREAMWORK

Two weeks ago, I had a dream. In the dream, my grandmother, Dorothy, stood before me with an open wooden box that resembled a box I found in her home after she transitioned, traveling from earth to heaven. When she handed the box to me, she looked like she was in the heavens, with lavender light around her. After she handed the box to me, she energetically communicated that I needed to make an offering to the tall oak tree that is growing in my backyard. This tree shades the chicken coop and runs, protects the honeybees, and has crystals on the south and north sides of it—rose quartz on the south and amethyst on the north. I awoke from the dream with a clear understanding and directive that I needed to make an offering to the oak tree, and I waited to see what the exact ingredients for this ritual would be. A week passed and sweet tobacco came to me. Fresh flowers did as well. I knew I needed to set up an altar facing the amethyst crystal on the northside of the tree, the side of the portal where the ancestors and guides await our arrival.

A few days after I had the dream about my grandmother, my friend, Katie, reached out to me about coming for a visit. Katie has a very sweet relationship with my grandmother. She has felt Dorothy tickle her feet in spirit before and felt drawn to items in my home that were Dorothy's, such as the beautiful ceramic bowl that sits on the island in my kitchen. She and Dorothy communicate with one another. I asked Katie to come and be part of the ritual.

Prior to my asking her to be a part of the ritual, Katie had just found some photos and images of her great-grandmother, letters about her life, and magical keys to understanding more about the ancestral patterns embedded in her bones and tissues.

The day before the ritual, I was in my car and I remembered that I actually had taken the handmade wooden box from my grand-mother's house and that it was somewhere in my house. When I arrived home, I searched for it. I knew I had moved it from one location to another. I found it in a closet, safely tucked away, and it was empty. Originally, when I found this box, it had in it ammuni-tion from my grandfather, a deed to the land my great-grandparents purchased, the checks they had used to pay off the land, and rail-road cards that indicated my great-grandfather, Willie Melton, had worked on the railroad and that his wife—my great-grandmother, Hopie—traveled with him on the railroad at times. Now, looking at the empty box, I wondered where those papers were. I remembered they might be in the bottom of a drawer in my office with some papers I received after my father transitioned from the earth, just three months before my grandmother. I dug around in the drawer and pulled out a stack of papers: my father's insurance papers from the National Football League, my father's discharge papers from the military, and all of the items I remember being inside the box when I first found it.

I knew this was all part of Dorothy's plan and why she came to me in the dream. She sent me on a treasure hunt just as she had when I found the handmade wooden box with family heirlooms and more information about where I come from. I opened the envelope with the photos and discovered two photos of Angie, my great-grandmother. I had no idea I had these photos. I found one very special photo of Angie holding me during my first month of life. She was looking down at me and I was looking up at her. The envelope also contained a photo of my dad in his military uniform, a few photos of him after high school and college graduation, and photos of my mother, Clara, at her high school and college graduations. I don't remember gathering these photos, and I am still not sure how they came to me and landed in the bottom of the drawer of the file cabinet in my office, but I'm glad they did. The timing of this discovery was uncanny given the ritual my grandmother instructed me to do on the north side of the tree and the ancestral stories shared in this book about Angie and other ancestors. It was clear to me that Dorothy wanted me to fill the box with these photos and place it on the altar during the ritual Katie and I were to move through.

THE RITUAL

Katie arrived at my house, and we shared a meal together. As I was preparing the meal, we shared stories about our grandmothers and great-grandmothers. After our meal, we gathered our items for the ritual. I set out with white and pink roses, sweet tobacco, a letter I had written to my grandmother that morning, a scarf that had belonged to my grandmother that became our altar cloth, the wooden box with photos, my father's discharge papers, a candle, Lambrusco, and a heart chakra smoke blend of mugwort, lavender, roses, and calendula. Katie had photos of her great-grandmother and step-great-grandmother, wooden bowls, a white candle, incense, sage, and two silver wine cups for the Lambrusco. We set out our items and sat down on a quilt that Angie made and my grandmother, Dorothy, repaired for me and gifted me on one of my birthdays. It felt like the perfect surface on which to sit as we gathered in front of the oak tree. We sat quietly for a moment as the hens clucked and watched the ritual from behind, and the honeybees buzzed around us. Then we transitioned into our ritual. The oak tree had roses and sweet tobacco strewn around it, and we poured Lambrusco at the base of the tree right behind the amethyst crystal. We sprinkled the heart chakra blend and I read the letter to my grandmother.

As I read the letter, I thought about all that the oak tree had seen and lived through and the fact that I just had ivy cleaned off it to allow it to maintain its nourishment. How interesting that Dorothy came to me requesting I make an offering to the tree shortly after the ivy was cleared off it. How interesting that she came to me with the empty wooden box, and then led me to find photos of my ancestors. Dorothy's signs aren't subtle; they are clear and profound.

MY JOURNEY BACK TO DREAMING

For many years I did not pay attention to my dreams. It was only the absence of dreaming that made me begin to explore cultivating a dream practice. I experienced a concussion in 2014 and my insomnia intensified. When I would sleep, it was as if my mind would go black and blank. I would awaken surprised that I slept because it felt like I was in the void. This indicated I wasn't moving into rapid eye movement (REM) sleep. When we don't enter REM sleep repeatedly over time, we can experience cognitive impairments. Going into the void in this way felt scary. I wanted to dream and remember my dreams. I wanted to receive messages in my dreams. I reached out to my friend Karla Michelle Capacetti, who shares a love of honeybees, to ask her about dreaming. I knew she had vivid dreams and kept a dream journal. She made a tincture for me, and I began to take a little every evening. I began to dream again and had very vivid dreams full of messages, magic, and information.

One dream was about me offering messages to others. I was in a movement studio that had two rooms, one large and one small. The people in the room were quite a bit older than me. I went from corner to corner of each room and placed candles there. I remember placing red, orange, and white candles—one each—in different corners, and now, looking back, I believe the colors connected with the chakras. The candles had paper messages on the outside of them, and the paper kept falling off the candles. Every time a paper would fall, I would go and replace it; I wanted the people to receive the messages. Then, all of a sudden, I was outside in the country on a beautiful day, going for a drive that felt spacious and expansive. This dream portended the messages in my first book, *Skill in Action: Radicalizing Your Yoga Practice to Create a Just World*, which I wanted to share with the world. I was writing it around the time of this dream.

I had a dream about being on a beautiful island. I was gazing at a set of stunning flowers that were on a stage. They were fuchsia and looked like bee balm. I wanted the seeds from them to grow flowers as well. I knew more seeds were in a cubby elsewhere and went to get them. I gathered the seeds and then shared them with some people in my dream. I showed them how to look for seeds in the flowers so they could gather them on their own. After this dream, I awoke to the news that the Global Seed Vault, buried in a mountain deep inside the Arctic Circle, had been breached after global warming produced extraordinary temperatures over the winter, sending meltwater gushing into the entrance tunnel. The vault, located on the Norwegian island of Spitsbergen, contained almost a million packets of seeds, each a variety of an important food crop. Remembering this dream now makes me think about climate change and destruction, crop failure, honeybee hives dying, the seeds we will need to grow our food, and the germination not only of crops but new ideas and ways of being.

While I lived in Portland, Oregon, the mountains seemed to enter many of my dreams. I had a dream that I was climbing a mountain but could not make it to the top. It was icy and steep. At the top of the mountain, people were there eating at tables, enjoying themselves, and I wanted to make it to the top. I would climb using my hands, which became icy and cold, and I would get close to the top but not make it. Then I would slide down the mountain again. People were rooting for me to make it to the top but the conditions were too treacherous. This dream is representative of so much of how I felt while living in Portland because of big life transitions, loss, grief, and a time in my life I would characterize as a dark night of the soul, a spiritual crisis for sure.

I had many other dreams and have journals full of them. Our dreams communicate with us and give us information from other realms about what we need to know in this realm, such as my grandmother telling me to make an offering to the oak tree. The information she gave to me in that particular dream led me to write her a letter where I asked questions about the time in which we are living and what we need to know to dream up a future that will be different for the coming generations. This letter is an example of bringing the dream world into waking life and continuing to keep the line of communication open between dreams and lived experience.

Dear Dorothy,

You came to me in a dream the other night and presented me with a box, similar to the box my mother and I found in the closet in the extra bedroom of your house after you transitioned from earth to heaven. In the dream, you stood in front of me and handed me the empty box, and without words, you communicated that I needed to make an offering to the oak tree in my backyard—the oak tree that shades the chicken coop and guards the beehives. My mother always said that I got my love of nature from Papa, your husband, but I believe my love of nature also came from you. I remember you working in the garden, pulling up vegetables, tilling the soil, and tending the land. I remember you talking about always having an "old hound" around the house as well. I remember your flowers and plants and how much pride you took in them. They made your yard beautiful, and how different it must have felt to tend the land and plant flowers in your own time versus working the land as a laborer.

I have a garden now, and while I had never thought of myself as a gardener before, I think I am one. How could I deny my roots and the gifts you and the ancestors planted inside me? On my birthday this past August, I planted my fall garden.

There was something very special about pulling up summer's remnants and preparing for fall. This rhythm is familiar to you because you did it for the whole of your life. You followed the rhythms of the seasons by inviting us into your home every holiday to celebrate being together, being a family. Ritual was important to you, as was devotion, and whenever I talk about you, I share how much you have taught me about devotion. My mother has offered lessons about devotion as well, but in a different way than you. You taught me about God, and you always said, "God has a plan." My mother taught me something similar about God's plan, and she shared that we are conspiring with God to make plans. It's not as if God is making all the plans; we are in relationship with God and cocreating our experience while we are here on earth.

This is precisely why I'm writing to you today. I know the ancestors know what is happening right now. I know you all feel the reckoning we are going through and, in so many ways, the reckoning that had to come because of what we humans have done throughout history. Dorothy, for over eighteen months, we've been experiencing a global health pandemic called COVID-19. It began at the end of 2019 and has continued to ravage our lives and disrupt any feeling of certainty over things. Over 4.5 million people have died worldwide, and I've thought about what you said about God having a plan. After COVID-19 began, news of the murder hornet emerged. It is said to be able to enter a honeybee hive and tear it apart, leaving dead bee carcasses in its wake. How strange that COVID-19 is leaving us death to deal with, and the honeybees we rely on for fresh food are at risk of being ravaged, too. I've thought about the plague and the locusts many times and sat in curiosity, wondering if what we are experiencing is God's plan.

Please know, I am not in the practice of questioning God, but sometimes, when things do not make sense to me or when

I forget I'm just part of the cosmic plan God is devising, I do ask questions, in particular about suffering. Grandma, I am curious to know why we suffer so much and what we can learn from you and the others about suffering. The systems of oppression you faced in your lifetime are in their death throes, and sometimes people fight death. You fought death, too. As I held your hand and told you it was okay to transition, your body would rise up in resistance. And then you settled and took rest. Systems of oppression resist rest because they want to continue to replicate themselves. The fear that we might imagine and create something so vastly different from what they breed is terrifying to them. When I remember we are imagining and creating something so vastly different from what systems of oppression breed, it brings me hope.

My question for you is, what do we need to know right now?

What do we need to remember?

I know you went through your own process of remembering because you would have been lost without the capacity to remember where you came from or how you came to be. You weren't lost. You were grounded and solid. You knew who you were, and you weren't going to change yourself for others. You would change yourself for God. How can we change ourselves for God now? How will remembering the divine essence of God within us and others help us change?

I have hundreds of other questions to ask you, and I will in time. Today I mostly wanted to tell you some about what has been going on and ask for your guidance. Not just for me but for us all. I am going to make that offering to the oak tree today, on the north side of the tree where the amethyst lay. I have flowers, the box you gave to me in my dream, tobacco, honey calcite, and pictures of you and other benevolent beings and ancestors. Your reminder in the dream was about giving back and about reciprocity. It was about remembering where we come from.

It was about lineage and legacy. It was about our relationship with the land. It was about opening a box and finding hidden treasures. Thank you for coming to me and guiding me. Thank you for loving me and being inside me, flowing through my veins and beating in my heart. Thank you for being you and being with us.

All the love and so many blessings, Dorothy.

Ase.

P.S. The hummingbirds have been coming to visit, and they feel like spirits we get to see in physical form. I put out sugar water for them to come, but when I put out sugar water at the beginning of summer, none visited. This time they are at the feeder throughout the day, gathering sweetness. Thanks for the reminder to offer sweetness to the spirits.

Reading this letter to my grandmother and the oak tree felt powerful. It was a tangible way of acknowledging my dream, heeding the call from her, and asking for support and guidance from the spiritual realm. In so many ways, it felt like an antidote to what dominant culture wants us to do—forget our dreams. Dominant culture works overtime to dampen our capacity to dream and vision about our future in waking life and during dreamtime. It thrives when we are unable to tap into our collective dreams for a world where we can all be healed, whole, and free.

Dominant culture wants us to be in a void similar to the one I experienced after my concussion—a void where it feels like all we can see is darkness, where we feel unable to access the light and energy needed to disrupt and interrupt the toxicity generated by dominant culture. When I feel as though there are no options or resources available to make social change and heal, or when I do not believe I can do anything to stop the horrors dominant culture creates, or when I am mired in despair and unable to connect to my imagination, it is difficult to dream about and create a new way of being. A way of being focused on our collective healing.

A way of being focused on us coming back into wholeness, being able to see our connection to all beings, being able to see our reciprocity. A way of being that prioritizes mutual care and coming together in all the ways we can to center the cultural norm of collective care.

WAKING OUR DREAMS

We need to remember to dream in our waking life. We need to remember to dream as we slumber, receiving messages from our intuition, spirit, and other realms. We need to bridge our dreams during dreamtime with our waking life, listening to what comes through the liminal space to support us in truly healing collectively and in community with one another. A plethora of research has been done on the benefits of sleep and the cost of little to no sleep. Less research has been done on dreaming and the effect it has on us during our waking life.

Recently, the intersection of dreaming and our well-being has been researched. Research completed by Matthew Walker in 2017 indicates that we heal as we dream: "It's been shown that deep non-REM sleep strengthens individual memories. But REM sleep is when those memories can be fused and blended together in abstract and highly novel ways. During the dreaming state, your brain will cogitate vast swaths of acquired knowledge and then extract overarching rules and commonalities, creating a mindset that can help us divine solutions to previously impenetrable problems."[1] We need to harness our divine power to come up with divine solutions to respond to the chaos and tumult in the world.

As Matthew suggests, dreaming allows us to blend together memories in abstract ways and engage in alchemy via problem-solving skills that are only available when we are in REM sleep. During dreamtime, we are not limited by our intellect or conditioned tendencies that are present in our waking life. Some dreamers, and people who study dreaming and dream interpretation, believe that when we dream, our souls are speaking to us. When we dream, God is communicating with us. If this is true, how could we engage our dreams to realign with the soul and our true nature? How might we engage our dreams to create a collective consciousness about what is in the way of us being free? Could our dreams and a practice of dreaming together lead us on a path to collective healing and liberation?

DREAMTIME

According to the geodesic dome company Pacific Domes, "Collective Dreaming is an ancient practice—our indigenous ancestors, wisdom keepers, shamans, and leaders, sought to arrange their tribal communities around ultimate truths revealed through collective dreaming or dreamtime. What's interesting is that these cultures did not separate waking life from the dream; rather, they sought to build a bridge between these two realms. Dreams were encouraged, shared and examined to help maintain the wellness, integrity, and spiritual strength of the tribe."[2]

Our ancestors understood the bridge between dreaming together and manifesting our collective dreams into reality. Many ancient civilizations had a practice of dreaming together and interpreting dreams. In these civilizations, it was believed that dreams were sent by the Gods to share information, foreshadow what was to come, or send messages and signs. Dreams were seen as oracles. In ancient Egypt, Egyptians kept dream books on papyrus recording dreams and interpretations of their dreams. Certain temples in ancient Egypt contained dream beds where people would go to induce dreams in the hopes of having a dream that would provide important messages, healing, or comfort.

The Greeks also had a ritual of dreaming together in temples. According to Snoozester's *Sleep Blog*, "They would abstain from sex, meat, fish, and fowl for forty-eight hours before entering the temple. They also drank only water. They would sacrifice an animal to the god they wished to see in their dreams. Upon entering the temple, they would then lay on the skin of the animal they sacrificed, hoping for insightful dreams."[3] Babylonians believed there was a connection between their religion and dreams. They believed the signs sent through dreams were powerful and they had their own Goddess of Dreams, Mamu. Mamu's role was to ward off bad dreams.

These dream rituals may feel far gone to you, and returning to ritual and listening to our dreams is part of what we must do to heal. If working with your dreams is new to you, I would suggest deepening your individual practice of connecting with your dreams. In this next section, I will explore how to build a connection to your dreams and how to practice dreaming together with others through a practice of Yoga Nidra. Before moving through the practices, I invite you to reflect on the following journaling prompts.

JOURNALING PROMPTS

- What is your relationship like with your dreams—dreams that emerge while you are waking or during dreamtime?
- What have you been taught to believe about dreams?
- Is there a dream you can recall that conveyed something to you about your true nature or manifesting something you wanted to happen in your life?
- Are there any rituals related to dreamtime you are aware of that come from your blood or ancestral lineage?

INDIVIDUAL DREAM PRACTICES

How we prepare for sleep influences how we sleep and dream. To prepare for dreaming, create a consistent sleep routine. Try to prepare for sleep at the same time each night and wake up at the same time each morning. If you have a favorite tea or tincture you like to take as you prepare for sleep—such as rose, chamomile, lavender tea or a tincture of mugwort, passionflower, or other herbal supports—prepare your tea or tincture and take it prior to getting into your bed or where you sleep. Gather any blankets, pillows, eye pillows, or sacred objects, and take time to prepare your nest for sleeping. Putting on a quiet soothing song or music with theta waves as you prepare your nest will aid the mind and nervous system in slowing down. After you have prepared your nest, get in it. Take a moment to notice how you feel as you enter the intentional nest you made for rest and dreaming. Here in your nest, begin to bring your awareness to our breath and to deepen it. Take a few moments to meditate and set an intention for sleep and dreaming.

SETTING AN INTENTION FOR DREAMTIME

In my chosen spiritual practice of yoga, it is routine for me to set intentions as I enter into self-study, movement, meditation, Yoga Nidra, and interaction with others. Intentions are powerful and serve as reminders of goals or aspirations we might have. Sleeping and dreaming are also places where we can set intentions. More restful sleep leads to REM sleep, and this is where we dream. Perhaps your intention is to sleep restfully or for a certain number of hours. Your intention may be focused on having sweet dreams, or you can request to gather information in your dreams. I have gone to sleep many evenings asking for guidance around how to resolve conflicts, interrupt writer's block, or meet certain ancestors or beings in my dreams. Set your intention and say it aloud or silently to yourself three times.

For example: "My intention is to have restful sleep and receive messages about what I most need to know now during dream-time."

DREAM JOURNAL

Earlier in the chapter, I shared I have journals full of dreams or tidbits of what I can remember from them. In my own practice of keeping a dream journal, what I noticed is that over time I was able to remember more of my dreams. A dream journal serves as a record we can go back to in order to notice patterns or themes that are likely showing up in our waking life through our emotional state or interaction with self and others.

While I was living in Portland, when I had several dreams about climbing mountains and not being able to make it to the top, it was directly connected to how I was feeling about my experience in life at that time. It was a challenging time for me, when I often felt confronted with grief and uncertainty. When I had a dream about my grandmother being very angry at a family gathering, it was about my family and the fracture that happened between my mother and aunt after my grandmother's transition. When I had a dream about snakes around my grandmother's house and then a huge snakeskin was found in her basement, this not only had to do with my connection to her but also transformation and shedding skin, which is exactly what I felt like I was doing at the time of this dream. Dream journals, like any other reflective practice, lead to more awareness and a deeper connection with self.

For your dream journal, I would suggest you pick a paper journal instead of recording dreams on your phone or computer. That said, I have recorded a dream in my Notes application on my phone because I was afraid I wouldn't remember every detail. After recording notes on my phone, I print them out or write them out in my dream journal. Pick a journal you like. I have a glittery purple one.

Place the journal next to your bedside with a pen and keep it there so it is easily accessible. If you awake from a dream in the middle of the night and wish to record the images, words, people, and the like from your dream, do so, because it may be difficult for you to remember the details after you go back to sleep again. If turning on a light and writing down your dream isn't feasible, you can use an audio device to record details from your dream and at a later time, write them down in your dream journal. If you awaken in the morning and details come into your awareness about your dream, record them in your dream journal. I have also had the experience of not remembering a dream until something in my waking life reminded me of it.

For example, prior to moving to Portland, I was there interviewing for a job. I had the job interview, got the job, and that evening went to sleep. I woke up the next morning to engage in my morning practice of prayer, pulling a tarot card, and journaling, and I saw a picture of a snake in the Airbnb where I was staying at the time. The picture jogged my memory of the most amazing dream I had about all the different stages of the snake that began with a large snake in a field, a baby snake, and then a snake bite from the baby snake on my index finger that sent me into a state of euphoria. This dream was all about transformation, birthing, allowing the bite to happen, and going through the journey of learning from the snake bite. After recalling the details of this dream, I immediately wrote it down in my dream journal.

As you work with your dreams and dream journal, if you find you only remember one thing from your dreams, start there. Record it. This practice will increase your ability to remember your dreams and use the messages in them in your waking life. Here I have described how you can deepen your personal connection with your dreams. Now I will share about dreaming with others. Having a deeper connection with your dreams in your personal life will support you in sharing dreams with others.

SHARING OUR DREAMS

I have found it powerful to share my dreams with others. Sharing your dreams isn't about asking others to interpret them. You know your dreams best. The practice of sharing your dreams can illuminate important things others might need to see, sense, ponder, or remember. Perhaps the people you choose to share your dreams with are receiving the same messages you are in your dreams. Perhaps they need to hear about your dreams to remember their own. You might choose to share your dreams with your best friend or one other person. You might choose to join a dream-sharing circle.

What I understand about our dreams and hopes is that if we do not share them in our waking life, they will not come true. If we have a desire for everyone to be whole, healed, and free, and we do not share this desire in some way with others and enlist them in this dream as well, it will be difficult to bring this dream and wish into being. Having the support of others to receive our vision and dreams, and to encourage us to conjure and bring our dreams into being is a potent experience. When we share our dreams with one another, the power to heal and move into collective action is magnified. As the dream psychologist Dr. Angel Morgan explains,

> There are many forms of healing in the world, and dream sharing in community is only one of them. The potential for powerful healing on many different levels of body, soul, and spirit exists in varying capacities within dream sharing groups worldwide. No matter how diverse the cultural contexts are with dream sharing communities, one thing they all seem to have in common is that they severely contrast any cultural context based on fear.
>
> Dream sharing in community has happened for healing purposes all over the world, within various cultural contexts that embrace varying worldviews. Although worldview is not consistent from culture to culture, the practice of dream sharing is something many indigenous cultures from all over the world have in common, from one time or another, depending on the spiritual and political landscape of that era.[4]

The dream sharing described above is a process where people come together in groups to share the dreams they have during dreamtime. The emphasis placed on the theme of cultures who historically engaged in dream sharing contrasting a cultural context based on fear is significant. Dominant culture thrives off our fear and wants to keep us in a place of fear. Many people are afraid of their dreams during waking life and dreamtime. Many of us have been conditioned that our dreams cannot come true. Many of us have been socialized not to talk about things, especially from the spiritual realm, that do not make sense to us. Some of us believe that if we don't understand what our dreams mean, they are unimportant. Dominant culture downplays the significance of our dreams, at times making us push them away or close them in a metaphorical box somewhere.

YOGA NIDRA

This is precisely what Les Brown, a motivational speaker who seeks to transform the world, was speaking to about the graveyard and how many unrealized dreams are present there. What if we held a dream and vision for our collective healing so our dreams do not end up unrealized in a graveyard? What if, when we dreamed and received messages from other realms—like the messages I received from my grandmother—we listened to them and acted in response to them? What if we asked our ancestors to guide us and share what we most need to know now to heal? The practice I suggest we use to connect to our dreams while holding a vision for our collective healing is the practice of Yoga Nidra.

Yoga Nidra is an ancient practice to support practitioners in different levels of consciousness. In many settings where I have been invited to move through a Yoga Nidra practice, it has been described as a state of deep relaxation—a state where one is still aware of their surroundings and not fully asleep but relaxing fully to access things that are more difficult to access when the mind is active and turning with various thoughts. Tracee Stanley, a spiritual teachers and the author of *Radiant Rest: Yoga Nidra for Deep Relaxation & Awakened Clarity*, describes Yoga Nidra as

A practice that connects us to the natural elements inside of us. It connects us to our ancestors. It connects us to nature. Yoga nidra is a journey through the states of consciousness while remaining awake and aware. As we are guided through the practice, we are led closer and closer to the state of deep sleep and beyond to our true Self, or samadhi. But we also stay aware; we do not fall asleep to the beauty of our true nature. We are aware and aware of our awareness.[5]

If we can return to our true nature as Tracee suggests, and as I believe my grandmother was guiding me to do in the dream I had about her, we can move closer to a place of wholeness. Instead of continuing to feel fragmented because of the toxic systems, unresolved trauma, and systems of oppression, we can come together in our true nature, which is vastly different from what dominant culture would have us believe about ourselves.

PRACTICE

Yoga Nidra Dreaming

The yoga nidra practice outlined here is intended to be done together in a group, although this is something you could engage in your own personal, spiritual, or yoga practice. If you are part of a sangha or spiritual community that meets regularly, you could have the group leader guide this practice, or you could listen to the guided practice available at shambhala.com as a group. After the guided practice, there is a group discussion, and you will need to have someone who can open up the space for dream sharing from Yoga Nidra. This can be the person who convened the group or someone else in the group. You will also need a large piece of paper and markers or crayons for people to record response to a prompt after Yoga Nidra.

If you are leading the Yoga Nidra, begin by explaining the practice to the group. This practice is focused on our heart's desire, dreams for collective healing, and information our ancestors may want to offer to us at this time. Please let people know they can connect with ancestors in their blood lineage or chosen lineage. Tell the group you will guide them to build a nest for a calming pranayama practice and Yoga Nidra. Inform the group that after the pranayama practice, you will guide them into a state of deep rest for about twenty minutes. After the state of deep rest, you will invite them to awaken and journal about their experience. Then the group will share with one another. If you are listening to the guided practice, I will guide the group and provide instructions.

Please remind people they have agency and can decide how they participate in the practice. If at any point they need to move out of the pranayama or Yoga Nidra practice, allow them to do so.

Make a circle with the group, if you are in person; if you are meeting virtually, have the group imagine themselves as a circle. People will want a mat, pillow, blanket, and anything else that will allow them to drop in and rest and dream. If for some reason people cannot lie on the floor for Yoga Nidra, give them the option to sit in a chair or in another cozy spot where they feel well supported. Have people set up their space for Yoga Nidra. Earlier I described it as a nest. The place for this practice needs to be comfortable and supportive so the body and mind can find ease. Once the circle is set and people have set up their nests and made any adjustments they might need, invite them to get into their nest for rest. Begin with a calming breath such as Dirga pranayama, or three-part breathing, where you invite the breath into the body in three distinct phases and empty the breath in that same manner— breathing into the belly, ribs, and collarbone, and releasing in the opposite order.

Another calming breath is 2:1 breathing, where you double the length of your exhale. You can begin with a practice of equal-part breathing and build up to doubling the length of the exhale as compared to the inhale. Often people count the breath as a way of keeping track, but this is not always necessary. If you want to count the breath, count your inhale and exhale for a count of four for three rounds. After your third round, count your inhale for a count of four, and exhale for a count of six, for three rounds. After your third round of this, count your inhale for a count of four and exhale for a count of eight, for three rounds. Both Dirga pranayama and 2:1 breathing allow the nervous system to calm and prepare for Yoga Nidra.

Now follow this script for the rest of the practice:

Your body is in its nest, either lying on the floor or sitting comfortably. Feel your body lying on the floor or in the posture you have chosen.

Begin by listening to the most distant sounds and drawing in closer over time.

Listen to the sound of my voice and allow the sound to enter your ears.

During this practice, I will be guiding you to bring your awareness to different parts of the physical and energy bodies. It is okay if you do not hear every word I say.

Now allow your body to feel more supported by the earth and settle into your nest.

It is time to set a *sankalpa*, or intention, in the present tense. This sankalpa is going to be focused on your heart's desire and dream for our collective process of healing. Your sankalpa needs to be in the present tense, as if what your heart desires is already happening.

For example, everyone has what they need to heal and thrive; or we are healed and whole; or we are all safe, happy, and free. Once you have your sankalpa, repeat it to yourself three times.

I will guide you to focus on various body parts and move from body part to body part rather quickly. We will begin with the back of the heels. Bring your awareness to the back of your heels.

Bring your awareness to your calves, back of your knees, and hamstrings.

Bring your awareness to your buttocks, hips, low back, middle back, upper back, back of your arms, wrists, hands, and back of your neck. Bring your awareness to the back of your head. Now bring your awareness to your ankles, shins, knees, kneecaps, thighs, hips, pelvis, low belly, ribs, chest, front of your arms, wrists, palms of your hands, neck, and face.

Bring your awareness to the entire back body.

Bring your awareness to the entire front body.

Feel your body becoming heavier and heavier, supported by the earth.

Now feel your body becoming lighter and lighter.

Listen to the words I say and allow images to move into your consciousness:

Thrive
Healing
Collective
Dream
Vision
Intention
Freedom
Hawk
Sunlight
River
Sunset
Community
Together

Now imagine you are surrounded by your ancestors or benevolent beings. They are here to support you.

Notice who is here with you and share your sankalpa with them. Repeat it to them three times. Ask them what you need to know to make your sankalpa come to fruition.

Listen to what they have to say, and observe what they show you.

Once they have shared what you need to know for us to heal as a collective, they will give you an object representing this wisdom. The object may be a flower, crystal, book, box, picture, or the like. Take this object with you and thank your benevolent beings for their guidance and care. Notice how you feel in your body and how your heart feels.

It is time to come back into the space. Deepen your breath in your body. As you inhale, say "I am inhaling" silently to yourself. As you exhale, say "I am exhaling" silently to yourself. Do this eleven times and gently begin to wake your body.

Wiggle your finger and toes.

Turn your head side to side.

Gently roll to the right side of your body.

Press your hands into the earth and rise into a seat.

Take a few minutes to journal about your experience. Record everything you can remember from your experience.

After people have journaled please make sure to ask them to gather markers or crayons. Invite people to come up to the large piece of paper in the room to draw their visions and dreams that came through in the Yoga Nidra. They can also draw the objects gifted to them from their ancestors. Once everyone has been able to draw or record what came through in the practice, have everyone step back and view the collective drawing. People can share what they notice, how they feel, or other insights upon viewing the collective drawing. Now invite people to return to their space in the circle and ask them to consider what they are willing to do to make their sankalpa come into being. As a closing to the circle, invite everyone to share a word representing the action they will take to make their sankalpa come to fruition.

Take a few deep breaths together and close the circle.

This is a practice you can revisit with a group over time to see how the dreams evolve and to hear how people are taking action to bring their sankalpas into being.

My grandmother reminded me of how intertwined our healing is by bringing Katie and me together for a ritual in front of the oak tree. She brought me the box to make an offering and to not forget my place in the ecosystem. She invited me to dream in this lifetime so my dreams do not end up in the graveyard unrealized. I hope the practices in this chapter support you in realizing your dreams as well. I hope they invite you to conjure dreams connected to our collective capacity to heal with one another, in community.

The bee's life is like a magic
well: the more you draw from
it, the more it fills with water.

—KARL VON FRISCH

HEALING THE HIVE

In this chapter, I explore what it means to heal our hive. In my exploration, I reference lightness and darkness. I share them as examples of polarities and energies the honeybees work with, and polarities and energies each one of us embodies and experiences in the physical world—for example, the darkness of winter and the lightness of summer; the darkness of night and the light many of us experience during our waking hours; the darkness we might associate with the shadowy or unrefined parts of ourselves and the lightness we might associate with our true essence or nature.

Throughout history, darkness has often been referred to as something bad, while lightness has been seen as something good. These attributes of "good" and "bad" have also been assigned to people based on the racial hierarchy—in other words, white as good and Black as bad. In this chapter, darkness represents the time we are living through right now and the light represents the emergence of something new. Darkness is referred to as an experience honeybees have in their hives; lightness describes the experience they have as they emerge from the hive ready to orient to it so they know which hive to return to after foraging pollen, nectar, water, and tree resin.

As I share about light in this chapter, I am not referencing a light that allows us to transcend or bypass the current cultural conditions in our world. As long as we are in human bodies, I do not believe we can transcend this earthly realm. I do believe we can transmute the patterns, conditions, forces, and beliefs that prevent us from healing and moving back into wholeness. I believe the transmutation of what currently causes peril on our planet will happen through a process of alchemizing together and connecting with the universal spirit in all. In this way, I suggest we can heal through alchemy by recognizing our oneness and by dismantling all that is in the way of us remembering we are one.

On January 6, 2021, which has come to be known as the day of the insurrection of the US Capitol, I had a magical experience with a bee well before I knew anything about the insurrection. It was a cold and blustery day. I had been going out to the bee yard daily to place my ear up to the hives to listen for the low hum of them flapping their wings to keep warm. One hive had a really strong vibration, and the other did not. Each time I would place my ear up to a hive, I would hear the low hum and then a high-pitched buzz as if they wanted me to know they knew I was there listening to make sure they were weathering winter well.

On this particular day, I went out to the hive for my daily routine of listening for the hum and I saw what appeared to me to be a dead bee near the back of one of the hives. She had pollen in her pockets, and she was shriveled up. I felt sad that she got caught out in the cold, and I wasn't sure how long she had been there. In the spring, summer, and fall, bees often die as they forage. In the winter, because they are foraging much less, and especially less on cold days—and because it is necessary for them to warm the hive, and in particular the brood, they die in the hive. It is not unusual to see several deceased bees near the front of the hive or the undertakers bringing out dead bees, carrying them far away from the hive. I connected with this bee and felt for her. I thought, "If only she had been able to crawl back to the entrance of the hive and deposit the pollen in the honeycomb to contribute to the food source for the larvae."

Something stirred inside me as I gazed at her. I was aware the rest of the hive likely knew she was outside of the box and because it was so cold, they couldn't shepherd her back into the hive. Bees do not think of themselves as individuals but as an extension of the hive. I believe that, while they know death is part of life because their life spans are so short and they see the life-and-death cycle in nature as they forage and buzz about through the seasonal changes, they can feel it when some part of their hive is no longer alive and present in physical form. She was calling to me and I decided to take her inside my home and place her on my altar. This felt like a much better plan than allowing her body to remain out in the cold.

On my way back into the house, I stopped to show my partner, Charles, the magic I was holding in my hands. I revealed the honeybee with pollen, and he said something like, "Wow." His daughter was there as well and I showed her, and she said, "Cool." Neither of them was as captivated as I was about this special bee. I placed the honeybee on my altar next to a small figurine of Isis. This seemed like the most perfect resting place for the bee, and I knew Isis would watch over her.

The story of Isis is deeply connected to the Egyptian myth of Osiris. Osiris was a powerful king in Egypt. His brother, Seth, became very jealous of his success as a king and began to make plans to kill him. Late at night, Seth quietly entered Osiris's room, making sure not to awaken Osiris or his wife, the queen, Isis. Seth measured Osiris's body from head to toe and took the measurements to a carpenter the next day. The carpenter was instructed to build a beautiful chest decorated with paint and sheets of gold.

That night, Seth threw a huge party and Osiris was the guest of honor. Games, dancing, and singing were all part of the festivities. For the final game, Seth brought out the beautiful chest and said the first person to fit perfectly in the chest would win a prize. All of Seth's friends stepped into the chest and, of course, none of them fit because the chest was not made for them. The final person to step into the chest was Osiris. He laid down in it and fit perfectly. Seth shut the door to the chest, then he and his friends took it down to the Nile river and dumped the chest into the water, knowing Osiris would not be able to survive.

Isis heard the news and was heartbroken. She went down to the Nile searching for the wooden chest. After days, she found it with her dead husband in it. She sat at the riverbank crying. She did not want Seth to find Osiris's body before she could perform the proper rituals that would allow him to pass on to the afterlife, so she hid Osiris's body in the river grass.

Later that evening, Seth went down to the river in search of the body and found it hiding in the river grass. He was upset and wanted to make sure the body would not be found again. His anger led him to cut Osiris into fourteen pieces and throw them across Egypt. The next morning, Isis returned to the river with her sister, Nephthys, and her friends to perform the necessary rituals to support Osiris in transitioning to the afterlife. She discovered Osiris's body was gone. Isis then transformed into a huge bird and flew across Egypt to recover the pieces of her husband's body. She found all fourteen pieces and, with the help of her friends, she performed an act of magic: she put Osiris's body back together again.

Once his body was whole again, Isis and her sister and friends wrapped Osiris from head to toe in linen, creating a mummy. On the night of the full moon, Isis conducted a powerful magical ceremony and brought Osiris back to life. Osiris embraced Isis and offered gratitude to her, her sister, and her friends. Osiris shared that he would not be able to stay with them in the world of the living. Since he had already died, his work now was to travel to the afterlife and become king there. He told Isis not to worry about him; he shared that soon she would be giving birth to their son, Horus, who would defeat Seth and take the kingdom back. Horus would restore order and peace to the universe.

This did in fact come true. After Horus was born, he was hidden from Seth and, when he became of age to fight, he confronted Seth and fought him for the kingdom. During their fight, Horus lost his left eye, but his eye magically came back to life. The Wadjet, Horus's left eye, became a powerful symbol of healing. After some time and clarification of who should be the next heir to Osiris's kingdom, Horus became king and ruled the earth, while Seth was banished forever.

The honeybee sat next to Isis, and I set out to make snow globes with Charles's daughter. Glitter was everywhere and we felt magic in the air. I took a break from snow globe-making and went back to my altar to see the bee. I was surprised to discover she wasn't there. I had a moment of believing that maybe I hadn't actually brought her into the house or that I had dropped her on my way to my altar. Charles and his daughter assured me they had seen the bee in my hand when I was making my way to the altar. I was astonished, but I also knew I had placed the honeybee next to a powerful deity, Isis. I looked all over the house, and I went back out to the hive where I'd first discovered her. She was nowhere to be found.

After about ten minutes, I returned to the room where the bee had been and something drew my attention to the window—bright yellow pollen. The honeybee was sitting next to the window in bewilderment, with a sprinkle of pollen on the windowsill and her pockets full of pollen. My jaw dropped open. I thought, "She came back to life!" She did come back to life in a way, and she would most certainly have died had she stayed out in the cold. But what actually happened is that she warmed up and this warmth allowed her to come back to life.

When bees become too cold, they cannot move or fly. If they are exposed to temperatures below 41 degrees for long, they cannot move their shivering muscles to stay warm. Still, being a new beekeeper and being used to more dead bees around the hive in winter, I didn't know that if I brought this bee inside, she may come alive after warming up. While her body coming back to life may have been scientific (she was cold then exposed to warmth), I believe Isis had something to do with it. She performed a magical ceremony to bring Osiris back to life, and I believed she did the same for this honeybee.

I scooped up the honeybee in a jar, took her outside to the hive, and let her fly into it. All of this felt surreal, and it did indeed affirm magic was in the air. Meanwhile, the essence of the story of Osiris and Seth was playing out at my nation's Capitol: insurrectionists were storming the building, calling for legislators' heads, and fighting for what they believed was their kingdom.

It is uncertain exactly how honeybees emerged. They are present in almost every ancient civilization and mythology. They work between realms just as Isis did with the earthly and afterlife realms. They ascend high in the sky toward the light and warmth of the sun to forage and gather resources that support the entire hive. They are highly adaptable and have created complex and organized systems where each bee has a role and understands that their role supports the sustenance of the hive.

Honeybee hives are considered superorganisms because they work as one. There is no ego or individuality; everything they do is for the hive. While we as humans have egos and are individuated as part of our developmental growth, we are also interconnected with every living being—past, present, and future. Most of the *dukha*, suffering, we experience on this planet comes from the belief that we are separate. We are disconnected. This feeling of separation may come from the wound formed when we enter the world from the womb or body of the person who carried us until it was time to be born. The feeling of separation may come from a culture that says we are separate and conditions many of us to believe we are independent rather than interdependent. Feeling separate may come from us having been made to feel as if we don't belong. The experience of separation may come from having been separated from our homeland, ancestors, roots, and culture.

The belief that we are separate is a dangerous myth that arrests our ability to see how truly interdependent we are. This myth makes us build gated communities to block out folks we perceive as undesirable. It makes us disconnect from the earth and mine it for resources instead of treating it as a sacred space we are lucky enough to inhabit. The myth that we are separate makes us start senseless wars and incarcerate people in cells with bars. The myth of separation makes us believe we can live our lives on our own and that we should be able to do everything without help. If we ask for help, we are perceived as weak because of dominant cultural norms and beliefs about strength being equated with not needing help. Honeybees tell us something quite different, as the honeybee rewilding pioneer Michale Thiele explains:

> When we link ourselves to the bien (honeybee), we can develop a deep understanding of the interconnectedness of all life and connect intimately with our most fundamental questions. The bien emits a sense of warmth and inwardness. It can make us feel infinitely vulnerable. The bien invites us to see with our hearts rather than solely with our eyes. The inquiry into the bees will naturally lead to an inquiry into our own consciousness.[1]

Just as the honeybees remind us of our interdependence and interconnectedness, yoga and spiritual practice affirm this reality as well. The Bhagavad Gita calls us into recognizing our intimate connection with all beings, the whole universe, eternal realms that are beyond our manifested universe, and our own being's endless capacity to love. It calls us into remembering our connection with one another instead of perpetuating our own suffering by believing we are separate.

I imagine a world where we understand we aren't separate even as we might be having disparate experiences due to the identities we embody and how dominant culture operates. I imagine a world in which we as humans see ourselves as part of a larger collective with a deep understanding that whatever we do affects the whole; where there are no wars and we are not fighting over the idea of kingdoms or sovereignty at the expense of the collective's ability to thrive; where everyone has what they need and where we do not see ourselves as separate but rather deeply interwoven and connected. I imagine a world where we see a tiny honeybee who has pollen in her pockets and we bring her inside to warm her up because we believe her life is as valuable as ours.

I imagine a world where we operate as a superorganism, doing everything we do for the collective care of all beings, the entire hive. Honeybees nurse, create, build, forage, mourn, clean, prepare, make honey, and communicate. All these behaviors are part of the web of activity that is required to support the hive. Honeybees are part of a larger web, an ecosystem where they depend on flowers to pollinate and where we depend on honeybees for fresh foods. We all are interdependent with every moving part, energy, element, and being, supporting the survival of the entire ecosystem.

Isis was an alchemist who possessed the power to become a large bird who flew across Egypt to gather the disparate pieces of Osiris and put him back together. Honeybees and many species in the natural world are alchemists too! They do mysterious things humans could not ever understand even as we study and research them. Honeybees fly when it does not make sense that they can because of their anatomy. They make wax from glands in their bodies and build symmetrical hexagons in which they store pollen, nectar, honey and nurture brood. They make honey from nectar, which they gather from flowers and place in their honey stomachs. Once their honey stomachs are full, they fly back to the hive. Nectar is passed from the forager to one of the indoor bees and then passed on from honeybee to honeybee until the water content is reduced from 70 percent to 20 percent. After this process is complete, they place the honey in their perfectly molded honeycomb, cover it with wax, and store it for food reserves. When it is time to leave the hive and organize a swarm, they create a new queen and go through all the required ceremonial processes to swarm in the holiest of ways. They fill the sky and hum as one vibration en route to their new home.

We are alchemists, too. We need to engage our alchemy at this time, just as Isis did and the honeybee does. This alchemy will guide us back into our humanity and the process of healing together because *we are community*. We are kin. We are interconnected.

Much like honeybees, alchemy combines a practical science with deep mystical philosophical and spiritual roots.

Alchemy is an ancient practice shrouded in mystery and secrecy. Its practitioners mainly sought to turn lead into gold, a quest that has captured the imaginations of people for thousands of years. However, the goals of alchemy went far beyond simply creating some golden nuggets. Alchemy was rooted in a complex spiritual worldview in which everything around us contains a sort of universal spirit, and metals were believed not only to be alive but also to grow inside the Earth. When a base or common metal such as lead was found, it was thought to simply be a spiritually and physically immature form of higher metals such as gold. To the alchemists, metals were not the unique substances that populate the Periodic Table, but instead the same thing in different stages of development or refinement on their way to spiritual perfection.[2]

The transmutation of lead or copper into gold, or one element into another, to further refine it is precisely the power we need to harness at this time. This power will assist us in coming back into community, healing, and disrupting all that is in the way of us working for the larger whole—the collective—to sustain the hive just as honeybees do. Alchemy's assumption that "everything around us contains a sort of universal spirit" is one of the main truths we need to remember to move back into alignment with the value and practice of care—collective care.

Honeybees' alchemy is vast and includes a relationship with polarities—light and dark, warm and cold, the earthly and spiritual realms, birth and death, and more. My friend Karla Michelle Capacetti, a medicine maker and sacred beekeeper, says,

Honeybees spend most of their time in the dark, and then they go out into the light. They are psychopomps, which means that they are those messengers, those guides between the realms. They transition. They go into the dark; they come out into the light. As human beings, we do that as well. We are like a spark of life in that moment of conception. Then we spend nine months in the darkness of our birthing parent's womb. Then we come out into the light. In Spanish, when we're giving birth, we say we're giving light.[3]

We are experiencing the death of the climate, the aftermath of a global pandemic, economic distress, policies that undermine our humanity, and oppressive systems designed to destroy us. Karla talks about this as a cycle of the divine mother giving life, taking it away, consuming, and composting so something new can be birthed:

> A lot of what comes through as I work with Spirit and the bees is that the divine mother holds, heals, births, and consumes us. She gives life and she also receives life. And without that receptivity, without that consumption of life, she cannot give. And so I feel like right now with everything happening, there's this big process of decomposition. There's a big process of death. And it's really hard to say that word because it's so real for so many people, especially Black and Brown people. But in the context of the systems and the way the world is structured right now, I feel like there's a lot of crumbling and a lot of deterioration and a lot of things that need to die so that the divine mother can really consume it, transform it, and something new can be birthed.[4]

Honeybees have the capacity to be with the experience Karla described. They have an intimate relationship with the darkness and light as well as death and life. They take out the dead as they prepare for brood to hatch and begin their work in the hive. They understand and work on different planes and can hold a larger perspective than the human experience often allows. When the bees are working within the darkness of the hive, they are not concerned about the light; they know it is there. They are interested in doing their work to make sure the hive is healthy and growing. When they are out in the light, they know they will return to the darkness of the hive, bringing gifts of pollen and nectar. We've been working in the dark for quite some time. Some of us are newly awakened to the darkness that pervades through violence, oppression, and suppression. And some of us have known that darkness and barriers to our collective liberation were weaved into the inception and foundation of nations due to superiority, colonization, and settler colonialism.

Given what you might understand about suffering on this planet and the need for deep healing, what does it mean to work in the dark while holding the vision of giving birth to something new, or "giving light" as Karla shared when she spoke about the honeybees. I do not mean to talk about light in an esoteric way. I mean light that is connected to our spirits. The light that is connected to our souls. The light that emerges from the remembrance of our connection to all things. The light that comes from knowing I am more than this body.

In the Bhagavad Gita, Krishna says to Arjuna,

There are two paths a soul may take. One leads to further rebirth and the other leads to liberation, after which no rebirth is necessary.

The path of light, of fire and day, leads northward, to the good fortune of a pure mind and heart. This path leads knowers of Brahman to the abode of the Self. The path of dark, of cloud and of night, leads southward into smoke and obscurity, keeping the soul locked in the cycle of rebirth.

These two paths, the light and the dark, are eternal, leading some to liberation and others to rebirth. Knowing these two paths, the yogi chooses his course carefully and is not deluded.[5]

The idea of connecting to the alchemy contained within you to learn to "give light" may seem daunting or like an intangible process. It is true; we often believe our magic is elusive. The reality is, we all have the ability to alchemize, and we do it all the time. The physical body alchemizes to support us in maintaining optimal health. Our cells are in a constant state of transformation every second of each day. Groups of cells work together to conduct specific functions, such as forming tissues that create our organs. Our organs work together to create our physical system and the manifestation of the body.

The process of breathing is alchemical. We breathe in oxygen produced by trees in the natural world, and we breathe out carbon dioxide, a chemical trees need to survive. In addition to our relationship with the breath and natural world, changing the very way we breathe is alchemical. We can engage in techniques such as Bhramari pranayama, or bumblebee breath, to calm the mind. We can engage in Sama Vritti, equal-part breathing, to increase our capacity to focus. We can engage in Kapalabhati pranayma, or breath of fire, to build heat in the body. All these types of pranayama (breathing practices) are alchemical in that they change our mental and sometimes physical states.

Countless studies have been done on the power of a practice of gratitude to change the way we feel and think. This practice and magic involves the process of taking time to bring our awareness and attention to what we feel grateful for and to allow where our attention is placed in the mind to affect the physical, emotional, mental, and spiritual parts of who we are.

Taking five minutes a day to reflect on what we are grateful for in our lives can shift our mood and make us more compassionate toward self and others. This is alchemy, too!

We engage our magic anytime we are in the natural world, connecting to the elements—earth, wind, fire, water, and ether. The alchemy here comes from recognizing our relationship with the elements and perhaps engaging them to assist us on our path. When

I visit the oak tree in my backyard that is connected to my grand-mother, Dorothy, I feel her energy and protection. When I connect to the honeybees and listen to their buzz, their vibration reminds me of my own. When I bring my awareness to the fuchsia aster that is currently blooming in my yard, it shifts my focus onto something so beautiful that it is almost difficult for me to comprehend. As I watch the leaves on the trees begin to change color and move through the process of falling off the trees as fall predictably makes its way toward winter, I am reminded of the cycle of life; the rebirthing in spring; the blooming in summer; the preparation for winter during fall; the retreat and quiet that often happen during the darkest, coldest part of the year.

Given alchemy is equal parts magic, mystery, faith, and at times belief in what we cannot see or know, I invite you to consider all the different ways alchemy exists within you and outside you. Take some time to reflect on how we can bring more magic and mystery into the world to support us in healing at this time. Consider your relationship with faith and the belief that we can, in fact, transmute the current cultural conditions and heal. Ponder your relationship with what you cannot know or see and explore what it feels like to trust what is unfolding. I invite you to engage the energetic qualities of Isis and the power to put us back together again. To bring us into wholeness.

In exploring alchemy and your particular role in transmuting all that is in the way of us connecting to the universal spirit in everyone and everything, it is important to understand the identities you embody and how you are positioned in systems and culture. The shared language section of this book references the term *social location*. Social location has to do with our group memberships and where we experience privilege and oppression—based on not our own individual story of who we are but how dominant culture positions us. I invite you to take the time to consider your identities and the particular skills you can bring to the process of us alchemizing collectively. For example, I am Black, heterosexual, cisgender, female, middle class; I am a US citizen, have a post-graduate degree; and I am abled. These identities offer a unique experience as I move through the world of dark and light and invite me to consider how I heal from the experience of oppression based on systems such as white supremacy and patriarchy, and how I dismantle systems such as heterosexism, capitalism, classism, and xenophobia.

How might your identities support you in alchemizing change toward the goal of creating conditions for everyone to heal?

How does your unique positioning and experience inform the ingredients and gifts you will share as we alchemize together?

During these times of darkness, and in our exploration to find the light and remember our alchemy, we might find ourselves stretching physically, emotionally, mentally, and spiritually in ways we did not expect. To reimagine the world we will need to stretch in different ways. Deeply and profoundly. Joanna Macy says,

> You're always asked to sort of stretch a little bit more. But actually, we're made for that. There's a song that wants to sing itself through us, and we've just got to be available. Maybe the song that is to be sung through us is the most beautiful requiem for an irreplaceable planet or maybe it's a song of joyous rebirth as we create a new culture that doesn't destroy its world.[6]

We all are being asked to stretch at this time; to find our alchemical song and to allow it to sing through us just as the vibration of a hive hums through the multiverse. Perhaps we can sing a song together that will allow us to rebirth a new world or to remember a time when we felt our interconnectedness and knew the universal spirit in all. Perhaps a time when we remembered and felt the universal spirit in all never existed before. Perhaps we can create it now. We do not know how honeybees emerged. We do not know the full process of how honeybees learned to cohabitate and work together for the good of the hive. They adapted from solitary bees and learned how to be a collective. Perhaps we can alchemize all that separates us and remember how to be one collective hive—a whole and healed hive.

Can we "give light" and conceive of a different world while we are in the dark?

Can we give light to something better to heal our past, present, and future?

How might we change our metaphorical metal into gold through an alchemical process?

May we traverse the darkness and choose the path of light.

PRACTICES

Polarity Dance and Healing the Hive

To conclude this chapter, and your journey through *We Heal Together*, I offer you two practices. One is a ritual called the Polarity Dance. The second practice is an invitation for you to create your own ritual focused on healing our hive. The ritual you design can be just for you or be practiced in a group.

POLARITY DANCE

I first learned about the Polarity Dance from my friend Mekare. She is a bee priestess who helped me hive my first package of honeybees. She came to visit me and the bees one evening and showed me this amazing dance. The infinity symbol is a profound emblem for honeybees. They are shaped very similarly to the infinity symbol. *Infinity* means endless or eternity. It describes experiences that feel boundless to us—for example, how limitless the cosmos feels to us or how endless time and space can feel to us.

The Polarity Dance can be helpful in supporting us through a difficult time or a time when we do not know the answer to questions that are present for us. I invite you to practice it now as a way of not only connecting to your alchemy but also discovering some answers to how we work in the darkness at this time to bring light.

For the dance, you will need two objects. Often I use two crystals or rocks. I place one crystal about eight feet away from the other. You are going to make an infinity sign around the objects by walking and crossing over in the middle. Now stand behind one of the objects you have chosen for the dance and say the word "cold." Move around the object and make the infinity sign, once you arrive at the other object say the word "hot." You are working with polarities. Walk back through the center of the space, continuing to make your infinity symbol with the steps you take, and when you arrive at the object, say "night." Walk again, making the infinity symbol, and say "day." Continue on this way, calling out polarities. At some point, you might decide to change direction. Move through this dance for as long as you would like and journal about your experience after you've concluded the Polarity Dance. You can engage in this practice anytime you would like and discover new insights as you do.

HEALING THE HIVE RITUAL

At this point in the journey of working with *We Heal Together*, you've moved through a lot of rituals and practices, and it is time for you to design your own. This ritual is about healing together, in community. Your ritual can take elements from the ones I have offered throughout the book or from other sources. Please remember it is important not to take from other cultures if you do not have a relationship with them. Be mindful of this as you create your ritual. The ritual doesn't have to be complex. Simple practices such as bringing awareness to the breath and deepening with others, in community, are profound and ritualistic in nature. Rituals that involve connecting with the elements or natural world don't require that you have anything other than access to the outside world or images of the natural world. Rituals are sacred; intention and care are central to creating them. Take some time to reflect on what you now understand about healing together in community. Think about what you feel is needed for us to heal and design a ritual around that.

JOURNALING PROMPTS

In this prompt, I've provided some space for you to write responses as you journal your thoughts about the ritual and think about some guiding questions to support you as you design your ritual.

- Who is the intended community for this ritual?
- What is the purpose of the ritual?
- How do you want to feel as you guide and move through this ritual?
- If you are offering this ritual in community with others, how do you want others to feel as they move through this ritual?
- Do you want to include the elemental energies in your ritual?
- How long will your ritual be?
- How do you want to open the space?
- How do you want to close the space?
- Do you want to call in energies, directions, deities, or ancestors as part of your ritual?
- If you are practicing this ritual with others in community, would you like to invite others to call in energies, the directions, deities, or ancestors as part of this ritual?
- Where do you want to offer the ritual?
- When do you want to offer it (around a transition in seasons, a holiday, a certain day of the week, etc.)?
- How do you want to document your experience of this ritual so you can remember it?

I want to stand by the river in my finest dress. I want to sing, strong and hard, and stomp my feet with a hundred others so that the waters hum with our happiness. I want to dance for the renewal of the world.

—ROBIN WALL KIMMERER, *Braiding Sweetgrass: Indigenous Wisdom, Scientific Knowledge, and the Teachings of Plants*

EPILOGUE

As I come to the conclusion of writing *We Heal Together*, I sit in awe of the magic that has weaved its way into every word of this book. As I was finishing chapter 8 about Isis, Osiris, and the wonder of honeybees, I was trying to save two of my honeybee hives. In the early fall of 2021, two of my hives were literally attacked by other honeybees who were simply hungry and found it easier to forage for honey than pollen. Foraging for pollen would have meant engaging in a long process to make honey, and the robber bees needed quick sustenance to prepare their hives for winter.

One day when I was out in the apiary, I noticed more activity than I had ever seen in front of one of my hives—loud buzzing, frenetic energy, and restlessness. I noticed this in front of one hive and then the other. I realized hungry bees were taking resources from my hives, robbing them of their honey. Unsure of what to do, I reached out to many friends who have experience with bees to ask for support. I read at least fifty articles about how to stop robbing behavior, and I feel like I tried fifty interventions to stop it. That is an exaggeration, but I did try several different things to make the robber bees leave my hives alone. I reduced the hive entrance so the guard bees could more easily defend it, and the robbers marched right past the guards into the hive to steal honey. I put wet sheets over the hive, which were supposed to confuse the robbers. They just waited outside on the sheet until I would need to take it off again to make sure my hives had enough ventilation. I put Vicks VapoRub around the hive entrance, which is supposed to mask the pheromones of the hives and the smell of honey. I'm convinced the robber bees needed the camphor and eucalyptus in the Vicks to mend what was ailing them and making them rob my hives. I installed robbing screens, which seemed to slow down the robbing behavior but did not bring it to a halt. The robbers figured out how to enter the hive by crawling up a screen, down into the hive, and past the guard bees. I prayed, cried, and would awaken at night, asking what to do to stop the robber bees from decimating my honeybee hives. Nothing would stop this unrelenting cycle of robbing.

I was preparing to move the hives to a friend's land to get away from the robbers so my hives could recover and rebuild when something in my intuition told me to combine them instead. I sat with the voice that told me to combine them for a day and then decided this was the best course of action. I went out to both hives on a Sunday and told them what was about to happen. I prepared everything I would need for the merger and got the smoker going to smoke and supposedly calm the bees. (The bees never calm down when I smoke them.) I smoked the smaller of the two hives first. This was the hive that had been most affected by robbing. I opened their hive and surprisingly found more honey than I expected, plenty of pollen and nectar, but no eggs or brood. This led me to believe they were queenless, which can happen in a robbing event. The queen can get caught in the battle and be killed or badly harmed. I opened the other hive and placed a sheet of paper above the top box, super, of their hive and then lifted the heavy box of the smaller hive and placed it on top of the super. To say this was a meticulous process is an understatement, especially when one does this on their own instead of with physical help. I did it on my own because of the urgency of the moment. I put on the inner cover, fed them, and placed the telescoping cover on top of the box that contained the food.

I talked to them about what was happening, prayed for an easy transition as they merged, and placed smoky quartz, obsidian, amethyst, a huge rock, and Isis on top of them and left them to work it out. After combining the hives, I didn't notice as much robbing, but I knew I really wouldn't know what was going on until I would be able to go into the hive again.

A week later I went into the hive with my partner to see how they were doing. We had drawn out a plan because we had to rearrange bee boxes once again and there were so many moving parts—thousands of bees moving about. We opened up the combined hive; took off and rearranged boxes; looked for brood, larvae, and eggs; and caught a glimpse of the majestic queen. She was plump, healthy, and weaving her way through the worker bees. She was a glorious sight to see. We put everything back together in order and closed the hive. I decided to name the hive that was two and now one, Isis. I placed all the crystals back on top of the hive and added rose quartz. We walked away from the hives with our hearts full. We are now hopeful the bees and the entire hive are going to be just fine.

To have recently completed chapter 8 of this book and experienced the tragedy and brilliance of bees is no mistake. *We Heal Together* came from a place of knowing we need deep healing and to heal together because we cannot heal on our own. It's impossible. When we believe we can heal in isolation, it's much more difficult to actually create conditions for our healing.

It is not lost on me that I had to combine two hives into one for them to heal and have what they need for winter. It is not lost on me that as I was writing this book, I engaged all those in my community who know something about bees to support me through the experience of watching the potential decimation of my beehives. It is not lost on me that I engaged community to pray, sing, build altars, and make offerings to the ancestors for my bees. It's synchronous that while writing this book, and during the time when my bees were under attack, two of my friends lost their parents— one lost her mother to COVID-19 and texted me to ask for ease in her mother's transition to the afterlife. The other texted an hour later to share that his father had transitioned and to send ease for his father during his transition to the heavens. Both of these people were calling on community to hold them and their beloveds who left the earthly realm.

This story about the bees is representative of what the process was like for me as I wrote *We Heal Together* and what I have known for a long time—we don't have to live life in an isolated way. We were meant to come together and heal. We were meant to come together in ritual. We were meant to find ways to connect when our way of connecting has been upended by things such as social isolation and a global pandemic.

When I wrote *Finding Refuge: Heart Work for Healing Collective Grief*, it was a shamanic journey of great proportion. I had to go through all the muck that my ancestors assigned me to move through to bring forth work about healing so we can become free. I had to build altars and listen to the beings whose stories I had chosen to tell in *Finding Refuge* for guidance and direction.

As I wrote this book and now reflect on my process, it didn't feel the same as writing *Finding Refuge*. I remember almost every part of writing *Finding Refuge*, and I remember very little about writing *We Heal Together*. This reminds me of experiences when I have gone through a deep and potent process but remember almost nothing about the experience. I just see and feel the impact of it. This is how it felt to write *We Heal Together*. I moved through it with care and intention, serving as a channel for what needed to come through from my highest self to the collective. I channeled what was coursing through my higher consciousness and spirit-wisdom about what we need to do to return to our interconnectedness. It felt like medicine came through me and out through my fingers as I typed all the words of this book. Rituals dropped down from the heavens. The stamina to continue writing about joy amid so much collective pain came from someplace other than my body. It felt like Angie was with me the entire time, and I visited her grave for the first time in years while writing this book. There she was with my shadow in front of her and her spirit filling the air. Writing this book was a ritual of being open to receiving and transmitting the messages I received from Spirit to earth.

We are living through a global health pandemic. It is quite difficult to know exactly where we are—beginning, middle, or end. We are holding the experience of what it was like to witness utter disruption and chaos in the world as we watched Afghanis try to board planes to flee a country that the Taliban had once again taken over. We are responding to the continual wounding that emerges from systems of oppression. We are watching trans bodies under attack, Black bodies being lynched using modern-day tools such as guns instead of trees, and hearing rhetoric about "Saving America Again," which is clearly about saving just a few and discarding the rest. We are in the apocalypse, the uncovering, and there is still more that needs to reveal itself to us. As we build from what has been uncovered, we cannot do it on our own. The only salve that will help us is to come together just as my two hives did and be in community as we heal our hearts. I hope *We Heal Together* provides rituals and practices that you will work with for years to come to create healing in your community and, ultimately, the world.

The process of putting my heart's song into words is a privilege. The words flow to me from the spiritual realm and emerge in the material realm in the hopes of benefiting us all. In the hopes of finding freedom together. In the hopes of walking each other home, together. I hope this book has moved you as it has moved me.

I hope you fall to the floor, literally or figuratively, as you feel into your heart and the magnitude of what we are up against as a collective. I hope you allow yourself to be picked up again by community. I hope we feel how sacred it is to commune with one another and feel the holiness of being with others who see and can receive our hearts and spirits. I hope we remember ritual as an homage to our ancestors who practiced ceremony in circle with one another, be that in response to strife or peace. I hope we never leave anyone behind. I hope we find joy. I hope we make joy. I hope we are wondrous. I hope to be in a dream lodge with you one day, dreaming up what is possible. I desire for us to find our alchemy and engage it to heal our-selves and come back together. I hope we hold space for ourselves and each other.

We Heal Together is a call for us to do what we already know how to do in our bodies, bones, and bloodlines—heal so we do not create more brokenness in an already fractured world. We know how to heal, and the universe will conspire with us to heal if we recognize a healing needs to take place. Our ancestors will support us in picking up the shattered pieces of who we have become as a culture and collective and remind us to do the work to come back into wholeness.

May we heal together.
May we sit in ceremony weeping and rejoicing;
     making magic and weaving spells; laughing until
     our bellies hurt and dreaming up the world we
     know is possible to manifest.
May we hold space for healing to take place.
May we heal seven generations back and seven
     generations into the future.
May we heal our sordid relationship with the planet
     and be good stewards of the land. May we dance
     with mystery and make magic together.
May we heal together.
Àṣẹ
And so it is.
So be it.
Now it is so.

APPENDIX

How to Hold Space for Collective Healing

Throughout *We Heal Together*, I have offered different stories, practices, journaling prompts, and rituals. If you are someone who would like to lead these rituals or rituals like the ones offered throughout *We Heal Together*, this section of the book focuses on what is important for us to remember as we hold space. Holding ourselves and others in a space designed for our collective healing is honorable work and no small task. Preparation to hold space is key. Learning to practice mutual care for ourselves and others as we hold the space is essential. Releasing the energy that needs to go at the end of a ritual or time in community as a space holder is critical.

I often think about how to describe what it actually means to hold space, let alone hold people as they engage in ritual and healing work together. People who do not hold space day in and day out often have a difficult time understanding how much skill and energy it takes to hold space. When we choose to hold space, we are holding people, their energy, and the energy created when a community comes together. For people who are not facilitators of groups or who do not practice rituals in community with others, what I do may seem simple but also intangible.

How do you explain what it is like to hold energy? How do you explain what it is like to feel the energy of an individual in the group or the entire group? How do you explain what it feels like to let your intuition guide you as you hold space for healing? How do you explain the mystery and magic that occurs when one lets go of their agenda and instead allows themselves to be moved by Spirit?

For years I have reflected on where I learned how to facilitate and hold healing space for and with others. I am sure the qualities I embody as a facilitator come from various people, experiences, and places. I first learned how to hold space from my mother, Clara. A spark was created when Spirit, the ancestors, and various other benevolent beings came together to manifest her as she is in her physical form in the earthly realm. *Clara* means clarity, clairvoyant, bright, and clear. These qualities definitely describe my mother. She is a shining light who has touched many people during her time on earth. As a child, I witnessed her in her classroom with a watchful eye. I saw how loving she was to her students who had special needs, and how direct she was with them. Her directness and clarity came out in the most caring way. She set clear boundaries with her students and was in total control of her classroom. Even though she was in total control, her classroom didn't feel like a prison; it felt like a safe space. She was a safe haven for many. My mother taught me how to create a container for sacred work and practice where people feel held, seen, cared for, and supported. She was the first facilitator I observed, and her skill is present with me every time I hold space.

I have observed others facilitate and hold space for healing in church, as I watched my mother gather with friends she has now known for over forty years each month as they played pinochle and talked about marriages, divorces, children, and the trauma in the world. I watched how my college professors held space; some of them did a stellar job while others did a dreadful job of facilitating conversation and discussion with their students. While in graduate school, I attended many workshops as I was preparing to become a social worker, and I watched facilitators and space holders who could hold the attention of the attendees, captivating them with story and their skill of building a space where vulnerability could be shared and received with care. I have attended many workshops, immersions, and experiences focused on self-actualization that have transformed me or made me very angry because of the lack of diversity within them and the assumption that we all self-actualize in one prescribed way.

I learned how to facilitate from my Dismantling Racism colleagues, all of whom are skilled space holders and spectacular humans. Each one of them brought different gifts to our collective. The gifts included art, music, ritual, practice, movement, the skills of interrupting harm and working toward repair, acknowledgment of the land on which we stood each time we facilitated, humor, laughter, beauty, transparency, and skillful sharing from their social locations. I learned most of what I know from them about holding space, and in so many ways, we brought ritual into the spaces we held—be that building an altar to begin our time together, taking a moment to center and meditate, tuning in to the body during times of disruption or discomfort, visioning and dreaming the world in which we wanted to live into being, and engaging contemplative practices for deeper reflection.

I learned how to facilitate from yoga and spiritual teachers who hold space for healing—teachers who know the practice of movement is a ritual and know that how we guide people to move through an experience can shape how they move outside of our teaching or ritual space. Working with the nervous system and subtler layers of who someone is, is a delicate practice and can either invite someone to settle into themselves more or recoil from parts of who they believe themselves to be. Often moving people in the way I am speaking of now feels like a balancing act. When working with Spirit, we are not just attending to the mind or intellect; we are working with the heart and essence of who someone is and calling them back into themselves and their true nature. The teachings I learned from various spiritual teachers taught me how to work with Spirit more deeply and move people with more profundity and depth.

Holding space takes an immense amount of energy. It involves a lot of listening, pausing, reflecting, witnessing, and checking in with oneself. Holding space for facilitation of content can feel very different from holding space for ritual; in both spaces, and whenever we come together in a group with intention, the way in which we come together can be a ritual in itself. Coming together in circle—be that virtual or in person, is the first ritual in which we engage.

The ritual of coming together was the impetus for this book. The need to come together was what drove me to explore the different aspects of how we come together and why we need to come together at this time. Every ritual and practice offered in *We Heal Together* focuses on how we come together. What is described below are different things to consider as you prepare to hold space.

SET AN INTENTION

As a space holder, take time to set an intention about the space you want to create or cocreate. Take time to think about the great task of bringing people together and with care. Reflect on how you want to do this. Would you like people to enter the space in which you are facilitating in sacred silence as an invitation to practice reverence? Would you like for people to enter the space in which you are facilitating as you play music in the background and invite them to settle in for a moment? Do you want to have people come in and take intentional time to gather and then open the space? What is your hope for the space you will hold for healing? How do you want the space to feel to yourself and others? What would you like to take place in the space?

BECOME AN EMPTY VESSEL

Become an empty vessel as you prepare to hold space. One of my friends commented on how I hold space. She said, "You must empty yourself out before holding space. You allow people to show up as they are and the only way this is possible is because of a practice of clearing yourself out to hold the immensity of what will inevitably show up in the spaces you hold." Yes, it is true; I empty myself out because what I end up holding in so many of the spaces I facilitate is participants' grief, dissonance, discomfort, heavy emotions, and suffering. I hold all these things while striving to create an experience where participants can be with whatever it is they need to be with, providing an opportunity for transformation.

Emptying out comes from clearing my mind and space as part of my preparation to hold healing space. Often the clearing happens through meditation, burning mugwort or cedar, centering myself, physically grounding on the earth, or writing down my intention for the space. These practices aid and ground me as I enter into spaces with the intention of offering solid ground to others.

FLOW

Most rituals and facilitated experiences of group healing have a specific flow to them. Many of the rituals and exercises in *We Heal Together* begin with an opening, some agreements or guidelines if the ritual calls for this, a practice, reflections, and a closing. As you hold space, and after you have emptied yourself out to be a channel and vessel for what needs to move through, take time to consider how you want to open the circle. There are many ways to open space. You can open by offering a centering practice such as a meditation, calling in, for example, the directions, elements, energies, deities, and/or ancestors. Plan for an intentional opening to signify the potency of coming together for an intended purpose and practice.

AGREEMENTS/GUIDELINES/GUIDEPOSTS

Agreements and guidelines are the posts that hold the container for facilitated practice and transformation. They allow people to know there are some boundaries and expectations of them while in the space. If I am facilitating a workshop, I always offer agreements and guidelines. I do not always offer agreements when I am facilitating spiritual practices or rituals. In these settings, I do take time to prepare the container and set the tone for our time together. The agreements I tend to use most often are a conglomerate of agreements I've learned over the years from various facilitators and guides.

SPEAK FROM YOUR OWN EXPERIENCE

Dominant culture has conditioned some of us to believe we are all having the same experience. We are not. Dominant culture has positioned some people to believe they can speak for others and, in fact, know the lived experience of others. We only know what we have embodied and endured or experienced in our bodies. We do not know what it is like to live with someone else's identities if we do not embody these identities ourselves. For example, I do not know what it is like to live undocumented in the United States and to face deportation, detention centers, or unjust immigration policies. From an embodied place, I do understand enslavement, and I carry the history of my ancestors' bodies having been controlled, tortured, lynched, and oppressed. What I understand in my body is resonant with what some undocumented people are experiencing at this time, but it is not exactly the same. I cannot speak to the experience an undocumented person is having in the United States. Speaking from our own experience means we speak from what we know or have experienced thus far. There are a few ways to practice this agreement, but the simplest way is to use "I" when one is speaking: "I understand...," "I know...," "I feel..." This is not an invitation to take up space or be entrenched in one's ego; it is a way of stating you are speaking for yourself and from something you know.

LISTEN TO UNDERSTAND

Listening is a crucial skill in life. Dominant culture has conditioned many of us not to truly listen to ourselves or others. Listening to understand is a practice of listening to someone else's experience while seeking to understand them more fully. I do not always understand what others share with me, and what gets in the way of me listening in the first place is the way dominant culture has taught me to listen. Dominant culture has taught me to listen for affirmation and validation; I have been conditioned to listen for whether what someone is sharing with me is true or false, right or wrong, or good or bad. I have been taught to listen while thinking of what I might want to share as a rebuttal or point of connection. Listening to understand calls us into truly receiving what someone else is sharing with us.

Many years ago, my colleague Vivette Jeffries-Logan shared a framework for listening with me. She described listening as a full-bodied experience. I love the idea of us listening with our entire bodies. Listening to understand doesn't mean we do not need to assert boundaries when someone is sharing something that could be potentially harmful to the group. It means that, when we can, we listen with understanding; and when harm is happening to the group because of what someone else is sharing, we intervene in a way that is responsive to the group and their shared experience.

ACCEPT AND EXPECT NON-CLOSURE

For many years my Dismantling Racism Works colleagues and I had an agreement: "Things will get messy and be raggedy." When I worked at the Center for Equity and Inclusion in Portland, Oregon, my colleagues' way of sharing this agreement was "Accept and expect non-closure." Both address the understanding that in a shared experience with a group, be it a ceremony, ritual, immersion, or workshop focused on self-actualization, things will get messy and not everything will be wrapped up in a neat bow with sparkles at the end of the time together. We live in a culture that wants us to package everything in a neat container—our emotions, experiences, pain, suffering, joy, conflict, history, and more. We are complex beings with sorted, vast, and intertwined histories. We move in the world with different identities, points of view, privileges, and experiences of oppression. Our very existence as human beings isn't neat and tidy and so our communication and experience when we come together with a group will not be neat and tidy. It will be messy and raggedy, and that's okay. Part of the most transformational practice I have seen in my facilitated spaces for learning and ritual is the way we wade through the immensity of all the chaos in the world together and the messy moments that are almost always guaranteed to show themselves when we share space with others.

BE WILLING TO DO THINGS DIFFERENTLY AND EXPERIENCE DISCOMFORT

I always share with groups that I might ask them to do something they have done before in a new or different way and they may experience discomfort. In ritual spaces, often people come into them open and ready. In facilitated workshops or immersions, people might come in with their ideas of how things should flow or be facilitated. As the space holder, I am willing to be flexible and to move with the group and the expressed group needs, and I will inevitably ask someone to practice something new or to practice showing up in a different way. For some, this may cause discomfort. Many of us know the experience of discomfort. We have felt or witnessed it or both. What I understand at this time is that being alive in my human body is deeply uncomfortable. Witnessing the onslaught of suffering and the impact of unprocessed and unattended trauma is uncomfortable. Seeing atrocities occur and not being able to stop them is uncomfortable. Watching the planet suffer and burn is uncomfortable. Living in a white supremacy culture is uncomfortable. Living out the legacy of systems of oppression is uncomfortable. To assume I can move through the world without experiencing discomfort is my ego rearing the shadow part of itself, telling me that I deserve to move through the world without discomfort. In our healing spaces, the goal is not to cultivate more discomfort. Rather, as you set the tone for the gathering, it is your responsibility to share that discomfort may emerge. Not because you want it to but because you understand discomfort as being part of what it means to be alive at this time. Experiencing discomfort is part of the transformational practice and process we must move through to transmute the suffering on this planet.

CONFIDENTIALITY

Coming together with others for practice, ritual, and healing is sacred. It is important we and the people who have chosen to come together with us all hold the space with care. One way we practice this is to make an oath to keep what is shared in the space there. I have participated in many rituals that have deeply transformed my very being. I love sharing about how I have changed because of sharing space with others and especially in spaces focused on our collective healing. It is not appropriate for me to explain someone else's transformation or experience without their permission. As a space holder, I can share my experience of witnessing someone else transform without disclosing personal details about them. Or I can share what it is like to witness a group harness power and energy to create and affect great change. It is important to keep what is shared, created, and said in our healing spaces in those spaces. Treat the spaces you are in as sacred. Hold and honor those spaces through a practice of confidentiality.

SAFER SPACE

Safer space was a concept that was shared with me through my work with Dismantling Racism Works. As facilitators, we understood the world isn't safe, and we wanted to find a way to articulate this to participants who attended our workshops. We also understood spaces that seemed safe could become unsafe within seconds. We learned the term *safer space* and, with the permission of Marin Burton, offered this explanation of safer space in our workshops.

> Safer space is a place where people can come as they are to discover, assert, and empower their voices. Safer space is a place where people can come as they are to encounter and listen deeply to the voices of others. Safer space is grounded in respect; it is a place where we assume positive intent. People

within safer spaces are working toward developing trust over time and are seeking to understand first. Safer spaces require continual work and mindfulness. A seemingly safe space can turn unsafe within moments. How we handle those moments is what really determines the safety of the space. Spaces are safer when we take responsibility for what we say, feel, and think to the extent that we can and when we admit that we cannot when that is the case.[1]

In so many ways, this speaks to the entire list of agreements and guidelines I have offered you in this appendix. The agreements offer us tools for how we respond when a space becomes unsafe.

As you hold space—be that for ritual, ceremony, or the facilitation of content, share about a safer space. Let people in these spaces know the conditions in the world have not yet changed in a way that allows us all to feel safe. For now, we are cultivating a safer space in the hopes of one day creating conditions for everyone to feel safe as they navigate their lives.

These agreements are ones that I routinely use. You might have other agreements you want to add to this list or different ways of articulating these practices. Take time to digest the agreements offered here. Work with them in your daily life and see how they feel and shift your experience with self and others. They are impactful practices, and making a commitment to work with them in an intentional way is a ritual that could change for the better how we are with one another.

Due to the nature and content of many of the practices offered in *We Heal Together*, I have not instructed you to offer agreements every time you come together. There are a few practices where I suggest you include the sharing of agreements. In any space you hold, I invite you to consider how you will set the tone and create a space for healing—be that through the agreements listed here or in other ways. When I come together with others for a ceremony or ritual, it is a bit different from when I lead a workshop. Use your judgment and discern what is needed based on the kind of space you are creating.

PRACTICE

After you set the tone of the space by clearing yourself out to be a channel for the experience and sharing any guidelines you might have for the group, move into the practice. I have offered several transformational practices in *We Heal Together*. Prior to coming together with others, decide what the specific transformational practice will be in the space, knowing transformation will occur throughout the entire time you spend in circle with others. Use the practices I offered in this book as guides and create your own. There are no rules about transformative practices other than to be mindful of where the practices you want to offer originated and investigating whether or not you are the appropriate person to offer the ritual or experience based on your lived experiences thus far—that is, avoid appropriating practices. And remember, when we come together with group and are holding the space, the experience might change us but the focus is on the group and how they change as a result of the container we have set up for and with them.

REFLECTION/SHARING

In many spaces of which I have been a part, held, or facilitated, time is offered for reflection and sharing. This is a way for individuals in the circle or group to witness one another, hear where there is resonance, and learn from others in the space. You can offer time for reflection in many ways, and I have offered different strategies for reflection throughout this book and the practices I've included. Make some space for people to share about the experience they have had in the space. Transformation continues during this phase of the process. When I sat in a women's shamanic circle in Portland, Oregon, over the course of a year, we would open the circle by sharing, then move into our transformational practice and shamanic journey; after the journey, there would be space for us to share. I cannot begin to tell you the number of times something came up in someone's shamanic journey that had also emerged in mine. In this way, the journey continued, and this circle became not only a healing space but also a space for learning. Consider how you want people to share and reflect, and create different points to share and reflect throughout the experience.

INTENTIONAL CLOSING OF THE CIRCLE

Closing a space with intention is almost as important as how we open the space. In the rituals offered throughout *We Heal Together*, there is always an intentional closing whether that be blowing out the candles, saying a prayer or blessing, or having the group reflect on their shared experience. If you open space by calling in energies, elements, deities, ancestors, etc. take time to close the space by inviting any energies that are benevolent to stay with you if they choose and any malevolent energies to leave the space. You can say something like: I invite the benevolent beings who supported our space today to stay if they choose and any energies that are malevolent to leave the space. This is to make sure energies are not staying with you or others once the circle is closed. You can close the space with a moment of silence, a song, prayer, or blessing. You can close by pulling a divination card and sharing the interpretation of it with the group as a way of acknowledging the final bit of wisdom that wants to be expressed in the space.

There are many ways to close the circle and the point is to make sure to do it with intention instead of leaving it open. While circles are infinite, often our time for ritual or a shared experience is not. Closing the circle marks the end of something and perhaps the beginning of something else. While non-closure in the form of questions or insights will continue to be present with circle participants, closing the circle does provide closure to the time and space people have shared together.

FIERCE COMPASSION

The two characteristics people use to describe me, especially when I am facilitating or holding healing space, are *graceful* and *fiercely compassionate*. It is true; I am able to extend oodles of grace and loving compassion with directness and clarity. I have clear boundaries in my facilitation and holding space for healing and ethics that guide me in my practice of holding space for healing. I want people to feel as if they are being seen in my spaces, and I also want people to recognize that when we come together in community, we are cocreating a space. Providing an opportunity for people to show up as they are while encouraging them to remember they are sharing space with others is fundamental. Creating a space where the group can cocreate with the space holder while the space holder or leader of the ritual continues to hold the entire group is necessary. It is no longer about one individual's needs when one is in a group. It is about the group and its needs. As a facilitator or the person holding the space or leading rituals in different spaces, I am also part of the group, even if my role is different as a space holder. I want people to feel as if they have agency in the space but not to exercise that agency in a way that is harmful to me or others.

INTUITION

In addition to my grace and fierce compassion, my intuition guides me in almost everything—be that decision-making, tending a group, or leading a ritual or practice. Bringing intuition into my space-holding has allowed me to trust myself and listen to the group more fully. While holding space, I always have an agenda or plan, just as I have written out rituals in We *Heal Together* with specific plans and outlines. My intuition isn't on an agenda. My intuition derives from a collaboration with my spirit, Spirit, ancestors, and energies to create an environment that can meet what is needed in a particular moment. This means I may change course in the middle of a facilitation or ritual due to what I am feeling in the room. My connection with my intuition has taught me to feel and see what is underneath the surface, what is between the lines or words someone shares and what most wants to be expressed and shared. As we hold space, especially space for healing and ritual, intuition and trust in ourselves and the group creates a wholly different experience as compared to when we are wedded to an agenda or timeline. While Spirit might have a timeline and things are unfolding based on that clock, healing and ritual practice often doesn't have specific benchmarks or time markers. We must be led by what is happening in the space while also holding the space responsibly, with intention and care.

MAGIC

I've facilitated experiences and held spaces where magic has ensued, similar to the spark generated when the universe conspired to create such a bright light like my mother, and I've facilitated spaces that have felt void of magic, usually due to the constraints of the institutions in which I was holding space. At this point in my life and career, I feel it is essential for magic to be present in every healing and facilitated space. Magic emerges from us working with Spirit, the energy in the group, and our intuition. It is an invitation for people to transform in ways they may have thought was impossible, and this transformation often occurs because of the particular group that has come together to heal in some way. I have observed magic happening in healing spaces when we go off-script or move away from our agenda, when someone in the group says exactly what needs to be said at the time or we take a moment in silence to feel into the space more deeply. Leave some space for magic and the unexpected goodness to materialize in the spaces you hold or of which you are a part.

SELF-CARE FOR THE SPACE HOLDER

The magnitude of what one does as a space holder is almost unimaginable. Given that we are holding space for others and at times for ourselves, it is important we take care of and resource ourselves.

Although I become an empty vessel at the beginning of facilitation, at the end of facilitation I am often full with others' energies, stories, grief, and revelations. While I do not intentionally grasp on to these things, they all come to me while I am holding space. A strong practice of self-care is what allows me to continue to hold space. In some ways, for a space holder, this explains the connection between self and collective care. I cannot hold space without caring for myself, and by caring for myself I am better able to care for the groups I am so lucky to hold space with and for.

For me, self-care includes the daily practices referenced earlier in We Heal Together—prayer, meditation, journaling, and the use of divination cards or tools. In addition to these daily practices, after I hold space with or for a group, I have a practice of taking some time to breathe into my body and release what needs to be released. I do not want to carry the weight of what can emerge from sharing time with a group. You can use other strategies to clear yourself after holding space: washing your hands with cool water, venturing outside for a moment of fresh air, saying your own personal prayer for closure and release, journaling about the experience, a deep exhale, and the like.

At times, we as space holders feel ungrounded because so often we feel the world in a deep way due to our sensitive and empathic natures. If you feel ungrounded, it is imperative for you to take time to do something to come back into yourself prior to holding space. You might still bring some of what is unsettling you into the space, and perhaps it would be transformational for the group to hear what you have been working and moving through. If you feel ungrounded and ill-equipped to hold space, I would invite you to consider whether other options are available to you for the specific facilitation or ritual you are supposed to lead.

Recently I was opening a space with a group I had been in community with for four months and I burst into tears at the beginning of our session. I was simply sharing about my day and how I felt and the tears started rolling down my cheeks. This is very unusual for me. I don't even remember the last time it happened prior to this moment. I asked the group to hold the space with me and for someone in the group to lead a centering because I could not. They did, and it was a beautiful example of how we can hold space for one another. I didn't ask the group to take care of the suffering I felt; I asked the group to witness me and then for someone to center us so I could find the ground again and lead the rest of the training.

Just because we are tasked with holding a space doesn't mean we must be superhuman in our efforts to create a pathway for healing in the space. In so many ways, my vulnerability, sensitivity, and empathy are what draw people into the spaces I hold. I am not a space holder who would like to be put on a pedestal or elevated; I want to be human, messy, honest, clear, graceful, and compassionate in the spaces I hold. I want to care for myself as I work to reveal my humanness in the spaces I hold, and I want the expression of who I am to invite others into their humanness. As mentioned earlier, holding space isn't an easy task, and while some describe me as a lightworker because I hold space in a way that elevates the consciousness of others to create conditions for our collective liberation, it can feel like heavy work. Being a container for some of the suffering we are experiencing at this time requires me to have a robust practice of self-care to release some of the weight of the world.

Given your roles as a space holder, what practices might you use to care for yourself? Holding space is a gift. Being in ceremony with others is sacred. Moving through transformational rituals often reveals the magic that is needed to transmute that which ails us collectively. Enjoy the gifts you will receive from sharing and being in space with others. Hold the experiences of healing together with reverence. Remember, we cannot heal in isolation; we must and in some ways always are healing in community.

NOTES

SHARED LANGUAGE AND NOTICINGS

1. Dismantling Racism Works, "Assumptions," *Safer Space*, Marin Burton, https://www.dismantlingracism.org/assumptions.html.

2. COMMUNION

1. Teo Drake, interview with Michelle C. Johnson, *We Heal in Community Summit*, November 26, 2019.
2. West Chester University, Tuckman's Stages of Group Development, https://www.wcupa.edu/coral/tuckmanStagesGroupDelvelopment.aspx.
3. Dani Leah Strauss, interview with Michelle C. Johnson, *Finding Refuge*, December 17, 2021.

3. RITUAL

1. Neil Vigdor, "Alabama Lifts Its Ban on Yoga in Schools," *New York Times*, May 20, 2021.
2. Aleksandar Hrubenja, "Yoga Statistics and Facts: 2022 Edition," *Modern Gentleman*, January 29, 2021.
3. Imani Gandy, "The U.S. Supreme Court Decided to Ignore Black Hair Discrimination," Angry Black Lady Chronicles, May 16, 2018.
4. Ali Isaac, "The Crow in Irish Mythology," https://www.aliisaacstoryteller.com/post/the-crow-in-irish-mythology-this. (As of October 2022, the site now appears inactive.)
5. Sherene Cauley, from a personal conversation about ritual.
6. Syd Yang, interview with Michelle C. Johnson, "Rendering the Impossible," February 11, 2021, *Finding Refuge*, podcast, 00:00:44, https://

www.michellecjohnson.com/finding-refuge-podcast/17-rendering-the
-impossible.

7. Juan Mascaró, trans., *The Bhagavad Gita* (New York: Penguin Classics, 2003), 6.29.

4. LINEAGE AND LEGACY

1. Alexis Pauline Gumbs, interview with Michelle C. Johnson, "Remember to Remember," December 15, 2021, *Finding Refuge*, podcast, 00:47:21, https://www.michellecjohnson.com/finding-refuge-podcast/2-10 -remember-to-remember.

2. Francis Weller, interview with Michelle C. Johnson, "An Intimate Connection with the Soul," December 14, 2020, *Finding Refuge*, podcast, 00:48;04, https://www.michellecjohnson.com/finding-refuge-podcast/10 -intimate-connection-with-the-soul.

3. Adriana Adelé, interview with Michelle C Johnson, "I Am Held," October 15, 2021, *Finding Refuge*, podcast, 00:46:08, https://www.michellec johnson.com/finding-refuge-podcast/2-6-i-am-held.

5. HONORING EACH OTHER

1. Patrisse Cullors and Robert Ross, "The Spiritual Work of Black Lives Matter," last updated May 25, 2019, *On Being*, podcast, 00:51:49. https:// onbeing.org/programs/patrisse-cullors-and-robert-ross-the-spiritual -work-of-black-lives-matter-may2017/.

2. adrienne maree brown, "unthinkable thoughts: call out culture in the age of covid-19," adrienne maree brown, July 17, 2020. An edited version of this full essay is included in her book *We Will Not Cancel Us: And Other Dreams of Transformative Justice* (Oakland, CA: AK Press), November 17, 2020.

3. Audre Lorde, "The Master's Tools Will Never Dismantle the Master's House," in *Sister Outsider: Essays and Speeches* (Berkeley, CA: Crossing Press, 1984), 110–14.

4. Race & Resilience, https://www.raceandresilience.com/.

5. Rachel Loud, "Loretta Ross on Calling in the Call Out Culture," Presidio Graduate School, May 10, 2021.

6. Rachel Loud, "Loretta Ross on Calling in the Call Out Culture," Presidio Graduate School, May 10, 2021.

7. Michelle C. Johnson, Tema Okun, Vivette Jeffries-Logan, "Accountability in a Time of Justice," Dismantling Racism Works, 2016, https://www.dismantlingracism.org/uploads/4/3/5/7/43579015/accountability.jjo.drworks.pdf.

8. Johnson, Okun, and Jeffries-Logan, "Accountability in a Time of Justice."

9. Johnson, Okun, and Jeffries-Logan, "Accountability in a Time of Justice."

10. Domyo Burk, "The Fourfold Bodhisattva Vow Part 1: Freeing All Beings," September 22, 2022, *The Zen Studies Podcast*, 00:32:24, https://zenstudiespodcast.com/fourfold-bodhisattva-vow-freeing-all-beings/.

6. MOMENTS OF JOY AND WONDER

1. Lama Rod Owens, interview with Michelle Johnson, "Reclaiming Care," November 18, 2021, *Finding Refuge*, podcast, 00:50:38, https://www.michellecjohnson.com/finding-refuge-podcast/2-8-reclaiming-care.

2. Kaitlin Curtice, "The Theft of White Supremacy," Sojourners, August 14, 2017.

3. Omisade Burney-Scott, interview with Michelle C. Johnson, *Finding Refuge* podcast, Healing in Community Series, November 26, 2019.

4. Allé Kamala, personal communication.

5. Kennae Miller, interview with Michelle C. Johnson, "Living Liberated," February 15, 2021, *Finding Refuge*, podcast, 00:49:28, https://www.michellecjohnson.com/finding-refuge-podcast/15-living-liberated.

6. Kelley Palmer, interview with Michelle C. Johnson, "Unapologetic Joy," November 1, 2020, *Finding Refuge*, podcast, 00:56:49, https://www.michellecjohnson.com/finding-refuge-podcast/06-unapologetic-joy.

7. DREAMWORK

1. Matthew Walker, "Why Your Brain Needs to Dream," Greater Good, October 24, 2017.

2. "Collective Dreaming in the Dome," Pacific Domes, September 20, 2020, https://pacificdomes.com/collective-dreaming-in-the-dome/.

3. "The History and Meaning of Dreams in Ancient Cultures," *The Sleep Blog*, January 13, 2011, https://blog.snoozester.com/history-and-meaning-of-dreams-in-ancient-cultures/.

4. Dr. Angel Morgan, "Why Sharing Your Dreams is so Important," HuffPost, December 6, 2017.

5. Tracee Stanley, interview with Michelle C. Johnson, "Radiant Rest," January 15, 2021, *Finding Refuge*, Podcast, 00:46:47, https://www.michelle cjohnson.com/finding-refuge-podcast/13-radiant-rest. See also Tracee Stanley, *Radiant Rest: Yoga Nidra for Deep Relaxation & Awakened Clarity* (Boulder, CO: Shambhala Publications, 2020).

8. HEALING THE HIVE

1. Michael Thiele, "The Alchemy of Bee-ing," *Natural Beekeeping Trust* (blog), *The Alchemy of Bee-ing*, February 1, 2014, https://www.natural beekeepingtrust.org/post/2014/02/01/the-alchemy-of-beeing.

2. Benjamin Radford, "What Is Alchemy?" *Live Science*, March 24, 2016.

3. Karla Michelle Capacetti, interview with Michelle C. Johnson, "The Alchemy of Honeybees," November 15, 2020, *Finding Refuge*, podcast, 00:41:53, https://www.michellecjohnson.com/finding-refuge-podcast/07 -alchemy-of-honeybees.

4. Karla Michelle Capacetti, interview with Michelle C. Johnson, "The Alchemy of Honeybees," November 15, 2020, *Finding Refuge*, podcast, 00:41:53, https://www.michellecjohnson.com/finding-refuge-podcast/07 -alchemy-of-honeybees.

5. Juan Mascaró, trans., *The Bhagavad Gita* (New York: Penguin Classics, 2003), 8.23-28.

6. Joanna Macy, interview with Krista Tippett, "A Wild Love for the World," last updated April 25, 2019, *On Being*, podcast, 00:52:07, https://onbeing .org/programs/joanna-macy-a-wild-love-for-the-world/.

APPENDIX: HOW TO HOLD SPACE FOR COLLECTIVE HEALING

1. Dismantling Racism Works, "Assumptions," *Safer Space*, Marin Burton, https://www.dismantlingracism.org/assumptions.html.

ABOUT THE AUTHOR

Michelle Cassandra Johnson is a social justice warrior, author, Dismantling Racism trainer, empath, yoga teacher and practitioner, and intuitive healer. With more than twenty years of experience leading Dismantling Racism workshops and working with clients as a licensed clinical social worker, she has a deep understanding of how trauma impacts the mind, body, spirit, and heart. Her awareness of the world through her own experience as a Black woman allows her to know, firsthand, how privilege and power operate.

Michelle has a bachelor of arts degree from the College of William and Mary and a master's degree in social work from the University of North Carolina-Chapel Hill. She has worked in several nonprofits and served as an elected official and on many nonprofit boards of directors. She has worked with large corporations, small nonprofits, and community groups, including the ACLU-WA, Duke University, Google, This American Life, The Center for Equity and Inclusion, Eno River Unitarian Universalist Church, Lululemon, and many others. Michelle published *Finding Refuge: Heart Work for Healing Collective Grief* in 2021 and *Skill in Action: Radicalizing Your Yoga Practice to Create a Just World* in 2017 to great acclaim, and she teaches workshops in yoga studios and community spaces nationwide. She is on the faculty of Off the Mat, Into the World. Michelle was a TEDx speaker at Wake Forest University in 2019, and she has been interviewed on several podcasts in which she explores the premise and foundation of *Skill in Action*, along with creating ritual in justice spaces, our divine connection with nature and Spirit, and how we as a culture can heal.

Michelle leads courageously from the heart with compassion and a commitment to address the heartbreak that dominant culture causes for many because of the harm it creates. She inspires change that allows people to stand in their humanity and wholeness in a world that fragments most of us. Whether in an anti-oppression training, a yoga space, or individual or group intuitive healing sessions, the heart, healing, and wholeness are at the center of how she approaches all her work in the world. She lives in Winston-Salem, North Carolina with her sweet dog, Jasper, and her bees.